The Super STAIN REMOVER Book

JACK CASSIMATIS

I dedicate this book to my wife, Kiki.

This edition published 1985 by Omega Books Ltd,
1 West Street, Ware, Hertfordshire, under licence
from the proprietor.

ISBN 1 85007 096 2

Printed and bound in England by Mackays of Chatham.

The Super STAIN REMOVER Book

JACK CASSIMATIS

INTRODUCTION

Running a home, keeping it clean, attractive and in good repair, depends largely on a combination of efficient routine, standard procedures and good old-fashioned elbow grease. Yet so often something extra is required. Even the smoothest running household has its unexpected spills and stains, those unexpected tasks that cannot be dealt with in a routine way.

The Super Stain Remover Book was written as a quick and easy source of reference on just such occasions. It contains a comprehensive list of stains and how to remove them, as well as useful suggestions for cleaning various household items and numerous other practical hints designed to save time and cut down the workload.

Magazines and newspapers often feature household hints, but it isn't always easy to find a particular one at the moment it is needed. All the information in this book is listed alphabetically, and it also has a comprehensive index, which means that the householder can find the answer to any query or problem in seconds – a particular boon in an emergency, when prompt action is essential.

While every care has been taken to check the effectiveness of the information in this book, the author and publishers cannot guarantee results.

STAIN REMOVAL KIT

Successful stain removal often depends on the quick application of the correct chemical or agent.
So that you may be prepared, it is suggested you store the following items.

Ammonia
Borax
Eucalyptus Oil
Fullers Earth
Glycerine
Hydrochloric Acid
Hydrogen Peroxide
Kerosene
Lacquer Thinners
Linseed Oil (Raw or Plain)
Methylated Spirits
Pumice Powder
Starch (Powdered)
Tailors Chalk (French Chalk)
Turpentine
Washing Soda

In addition to the above, store some clean rags, plain fine steel wool pads and clean white blotting paper.

CAUTION

Some of the cleaning suggestions in this book require the use of chemicals which, if not used correctly, could have various side effects. It is strongly suggested that where this symbol **CAUTION ▶** appears in the book, you refer to these "CAUTION" notes and follow closely the precautions suggested.
When not being used all chemicals should be safely locked away and high up out of the reach of children.
Purchase from your chemist the appropriate antidotes suggested on the labels of the chemicals and keep together with the chemicals in case of poisoning.

Acetone
Is highly inflammable. Keep away from any naked flame and do not smoke.

Ammonia
Gives off highly pungent fumes. Wear rubber gloves and avoid breathing the fumes. Wash any splashes from your skin.

Amyl Acetate
Is highly inflammable and its fumes are extremely toxic. Keep away from any naked flame and work preferably in the open air but if this is not possible, open all windows and doors and do not smoke or breathe the fumes.

Caustic Soda
Is very corrosive. Wear rubber gloves and avoid splashing onto skin or eyes. If accident occurs, wash off with plenty of fresh water and see your doctor if eye is affected. Do not use aluminium containers.

Copper Sulphate
Is poisonous. Wear rubber gloves and avoid breathing the dust or fumes and avoid contact with skin or eyes. If accident occurs, wash with plenty of water.

Hydrochloric Acid
Is highly corrosive. Wear rubber gloves and avoid splashing onto skin or eyes. If accident occurs, wash off with plenty of fresh water and see your doctor if eye is affected. When mixing, use only a plastic, glass or earthenware container.

Hydrogen Peroxide
Unless otherwise stated, must always be diluted with water. Refer to instructions on container.

Kerosene
Is inflammable. Keep away from any naked flame.

Methylated Spirits
Is highly inflammable. Keep away from any naked flame and do not smoke.

Nail Polish Remover
Is highy inflammable. Keep away from any naked flame and do not smoke.

Oxalic Acid
Is poisonous. Wear rubber gloves and avoid contact with skin or eyes. If accident occurs, wash off with plenty of water.

Thinners
Are extremely inflammable. Keep away from any naked flame and do not smoke.

Turpentine (Mineral Turpentine)
Is highly inflammable. Keep away from any naked flame.

FUNDAMENTALS OF STAIN REMOVAL

- The fresher the stain the easier it is to remove.
- Test chemicals for suitability on unseen part of clothing or fabric as some synthetic fibres or colours may be adversely affected.
- When using grease solvents first apply away from stain and work towards the centre. This will help prevent a ring forming. Only use clean cloths.
- When using commercial products make sure you follow directions and precautions on container.
- Treat acids with care. Use rubber gloves.
- Some cleaning fluids evaporate quickly and do not allow enough time to clean stain. Overcome this problem by placing a cup or similar over stain immediately after applying cleaning fluid. Let soak then proceed with cleaning.

★Indicates an alternative method of treatment.

ACID

Washables

Spread on ammonia immediately to prevent burning a hole. Rub well with ammonia and wash as usual. Washing soda can be substituted for ammonia. **CAUTION ▶**

Acid on blue cloth or serge will turn red if not neutralized with ammonia immediately. If the colour of the fabric is affected by the ammonia neutralize at once with white vinegar. **CAUTION ▶**

ALABASTER

Cleaning

Make a paste of quicklime and water, rub over alabaster and leave for 30 hours. Wash off with liquid detergent and warm water and rinse in clean water. Polish with a soft dry cloth.

Stained

Using a cloth dampened in turpentine, rub fine pumice powder over badly stained alabaster. Wash off as above. **CAUTION ▶**

ALCOHOL SPIRITS

Carpet

As quickly as possible absorb excess liquid and sponge stain with a cloth lightly dampened with warm water.

Clothes

As quickly as possible and before stain dries, sponge with cold water followed by diluted liquid detergent.

For whites, rinse in cold water with a few drops of white vinegar added and wash as usual.

For coloureds, use hydrogen peroxide instead of white vinegar. If still stained when garment is dry, sponge with pure alcohol.

Polished Wood

Rub gently with a cloth moistened with linseed oil and use cigarette or cigar ash as a mild abrasive.

*Mix linseed oil and pumice powder into a thin paste. Rub in direction of grain and wipe off with plain linseed oil. Follow with furniture polish. May have to be repeated.

*Rub lightly with silver polish.

ALUMINIUM

Abrasive Cleaner

Grate a cake of bath soap into 1¼ cups (10 fl oz) of water and slowly heat till the soap melts and forms a jelly. Remove from heat, add ¼ cup (2 fl oz) of turpentine and while beating with an electric mixer, slowly add 6 teaspoons of fine emery powder. Store in a sealed jar and use with a soft cloth. **CAUTION ▶**

Non-abrasive Cleaner

Grate a cake of bath soap into 2 cups (16 fl oz) of water and slowly heat till the soap melts and forms a jelly. Remove from heat, add ½ cup (2½ oz) of borax and reheat. Remove from heat while still a jelly and beat with an electric mixer at slow speed for approximately 5 minutes. When cool add ¾ cup (6 fl oz) of water and 6 teaspoons of glycerine and beat for another 2 or 3 minutes or until fluffy. Store in a sealed jar and use with fine steel wool. This cleaner should not pit the aluminium.

Polishing

Dip a dry pad of fine steel wool in plain (all-purpose) flour and rub evenly for a high polish.

⋆Sprinkle a liberal amount of cloudy ammonia onto a clean rag and rub gently over aluminium. Polish off with a soft cloth. **CAUTION ▶**

ALUMINIUM POTS

Cleaner

Mix equal quantities of olive oil and methylated spirits and rub well with fine steel wool. Wash as usual. **CAUTION ▶**

⋆Sprinkle cooking salt all over bottom of pot or pan and let heat for 10 minutes or so. Remove salt and wipe well with a paper towel.

Darkened Pots

Three quarters fill pot with water, add 1 tablespoon of cream of tartar and boil for 15 minutes or so. Finally remove any white residue with fine steel wool and detergent.

⋆Three quarters fill pot with water, add any acidy fruit peelings such as lemons, oranges, apples or even rhubarb and boil for 15 minutes or so. Finally clean with fine steel wool and detergent.

ANIMAL DETERRENT

Cats, Dogs
Sprinkle pepper on affected area.
*Bury bottles up to their necks in the soil and half fill with ammonia. **CAUTION ▶**

Snails
To prevent rain washing the baits away, put them in a fairly large empty food tin and lay the tin on its side on the soil. An added advantage of this is that baits may be removed when pets are around. If you're out of commercial baits, put some bran in the tin.
*Laying sawdust around is another method of trapping snails because it prevents them from getting back into their shells.

ANTS

See PEST REMOVAL (page 57).

ARTICHOKE

Hands
Cut a lemon in half and rub your hands with the raw edge. Rinse off in cold water.

BALL POINT

See INK, BALL POINT (page 39).

BAMBOO

See CANE (page 15).

BARBECUE PLATE

Dissolve ½ cup (3 oz) caustic soda in 4 cups (1 litre) very hot water. Pour onto barbecue plate and scrub with an old brush. Rinse off well. Repeat if necessary. **CAUTION ▶**

BATH OR SINK

Bath Essence
Break 5 or 6 roses into a small saucepan, add a little rosemary and a pinch of salt. Cover with water, bring to the boil, let simmer gently for 1 minute and strain. Add to bath water as required.

Cleaner
Mix equal quantities of kerosene and methylated spirits and rub over sinks, etc. with a soft cloth. **CAUTION ▶**

Preventing Water Ring
Make a small sachet out of cheesecloth, fill with oatmeal and leave soaking in bath. The oatmeal stops grease from sticking to the sides of the bath.

Removal of Water Ring
Mix 2 parts of kerosene to 1 part methylated spirits and rub over water ring with a soft cloth. **CAUTION ▶**
*A more effective scrubbing cloth is old nylon netting or the net bags in which onions are sold. Wrap old nylon netting around your usual scrubbing cloth or put 3 or 4 onion bags into 1 onion bag and use as a scrubbing cloth.

BEER

Polished Wood
Remove by rubbing gently with a cloth moistened in plain linseed oil and use cigarette or cigar ash as a mild abrasive.
*Mix plain linseed oil and pumice powder into a thin paste. Rub in direction of grain and wipe off with plain linseed oil. Follow with furniture polish. May have to be repeated.

Unwashables
Rub over with methylated spirits followed by hand soap. When dry, brush off and sponge with cold water. **CAUTION ▶**

Washables
Wash in warm water containing ammonia. **CAUTION ▶**

BEETROOT FRESH

Washables
Soak a slice of bread in cold water and place over stain. After stain is absorbed by the bread, wash as usual.

BIRD DROPPINGS

Fabric
If fresh just wash off with water. If dry, scrape off as much as possible and remove stain with a solution of dishwashing detergent and water with a few added drops of ammonia. Rinse off with fresh water. **CAUTION ▶**

BLEACH YELLOW

Washables
Make a solution of 6 teaspoons of hydrogen peroxide to 1 cup (8 fl oz) of water. Keep sponging stain until it disappears. Wash as usual.

BLINDS

Fringes
Work shaving cream into a lather and apply to the fringes with a nail brush. When dry, brush off.

Holland
Make the following solution:
In a 9 litre bucket pour 1/4 cup (1 oz) clothes washing powder, 1/2 cup (4 fl oz) kerosene and three quarters fill with warm water. Stir well. Remove blind from window and lay out on a clean, flat surface. With a soft cloth apply mixture all over blind on both sides, wiping off each side with a clean cloth as it is finished. **CAUTION ▶**

Venetian
Cleaning very dirty venetians
Make the following solution:
In a 9 litre bucket pour 1/4 cup (1 oz) clothes washing powder, 1/2 cup (4 fl oz) kerosene and three quarters fill with warm water. Stir well. Remove blind from window and lay out on a flat, clean surface. Using a soft broom or a sponge mop, dip into solution and scrub the blinds, including the pelmet, tapes and cords. Apply to both sides. When clean, hang over the clothesline and hose off all the cleaning solution. Leave to dry. **CAUTION ▶**
Cleaning without removing from windows
Wipe each slat with a cloth lightly dampened with kerosene. Polish with a dry cloth. **CAUTION ▶**
* Use equal parts of methylated spirits and water or liquid detergent diluted with warm water. **CAUTION ▶**

BLOOD

Carpet
Sponge stain with diluted liquid detergent and then with clean water. If any stain remains rub with a cloth dampened with hydrogen peroxide. Sponge with clean water. At no time allow the hydrogen peroxide to saturate the carpet.

Coloureds
Rub lightly with hydrogen peroxide.

Unwashwables
Mix cornflour or starch with water till thick and spread over stain. Wait until dry and brush off. May need repetition.

White Washables
Soak in cold salty water and wash as usual (1 tablespoon salt per 2½ cups (20 fl oz) water).
* Use household bleach as per directions on container.

BOOKS

Top Edge of Pages
Rub dirt away with an art gum eraser. If still soiled, rub gently with a dry pad of fine steel wool.

BOTTLES

Hard to get into Bottles
Pour into bottle a little vinegar, crushed egg shells and hot water. Shake very well and leave for a day or so. Shake every now and then and if still stained, clean with fine steel wool tied to a thin stick.
* Tie a thin chain onto a piece of string, drop chain into the bottle with hot water and detergent, seal bottle and shake well. When clean, remove chain and rinse well.

BRASS

Polishing
Use ordinary brass polish or automobile cutting compound. Apply with a soft cloth or if necessary with a pad of fine steel wool. Rub only in straight lines, not crosswise or in circles. When dry, remove polish with silk cloth and for a really high gleam rub with plain (all-purpose) flour. Flour removes all traces of polish and helps maintain the shine.

See TARNISH, Brass (page 70).

BROILER

See GRILLER (BROILER) Page 37).

BUBBLE GUM

See CHEWING GUM (Page 18).

BURNS CIGARETTE

Carpet
While the burn cannot be removed it can be hidden by rubbing around it with steel wool. This will lift the carpet fibres and cover the mark.
*First remove all burn marks by rubbing carefully with steel wool or sand paper.
Next pour into the burn hole a little clear, waterproof adhesive and with a pair of fine pointed tweezers, pluck fragments of pile from the surrounding carpet and push into the adhesive. When dry, tease patch with a small wire brush to remove any glazing effect.

Fabric
For light fabric, darn the hole with matching tapestry or crocheting thread. For heavier fabric use wool.

Polished Wood
Mix fine pumice powder and raw linseed oil to a thin paste. Rub over scorch mark in the direction of the grain. Wipe off with cloth dipped in plain linseed oil. Repeat if necessary. Finish off with furniture polish.

Upholstery
Mix 4 tablespoons of borax with 2 cups (16 fl oz) hot water. Dampen a cleaning rag with above solution and rub over burn mark till it disappears. Sponge off with clean water and pat dry.

BURNS POTS, PANS, DISHES

Method 1
Pour in hot water and 1 tablespoon of bleach and let soak. All food particles should then come off easily in the wash. For really caked-on food, place dish or saucepan on stove and let boil for 10 minutes or more.
*For old and really baked-on grease, saturate an old rag with ammonia and put it along with the pot or pan, in a plastic bag.

Seal bag and leave for a day or so. Wash as usual. **CAUTION ▶**
NOTE: This method may cause pitting on new aluminium.

Method 2
Three quarters fill pot with cold water and leave to soak for 30 minutes. Add 1 heaped tablespoon of powdered borax and leave to boil for 10 minutes or so. Wash as usual.

Method 3
Sprinkle salt, bicarbonate of soda (baking soda) or coffee grounds over bottom of pot, cover with vinegar and leave stand for an hour or more. Then add a little water, boil for 10 minutes and wash as usual.

CANDLE GREASE

Furniture
Wait till the drops of wax become hard (few hours). Place large sheet of aluminium foil over drops and on top of this place a hot steamy towel. Do not let the towel touch the woodwork. When sufficiently heated, wax should soften and you can peel it off. See also WAX (page 75).

CANE BAMBOO

Cleaning Liquid
Mix the following:
1¼ cups (10 fl oz) turpentine
¾ cup (6 fl oz) linseed oil
½ cup (4 fl oz) vinegar
¾ cup (6 fl oz) methylated spirits
Rub well all over cane or bamboo and dry off with a clean cloth. When dry, restore gloss by painting all over with clear lacquer.
CAUTION ▶

Quick Cleaning
Scrub with a solution of 3 teaspoons of ammonia and 3 teaspoons salt to 1 litre (4 cups) water and rinse off with clean water. Let dry in the shade. When dry, finish off with furniture polish.
CAUTION ▶

CARBON PAPER

Fabric
Sponge stain with methylated spirits. **CAUTION ▶**

CARDS PLAYING

Wipe each card, on both sides, with spirits of camphor and let dry. When dry, sprinkle talcum powder over each card and polish with soft cloth. A light dusting of talcum powder every now and then will get rid of surface grease and reduce the number of cleanings required.

CARPET

Brighten old carpet
First clean carpet thoroughly with vacuum cleaner and then apply with a sponge the following solution:
2 parts water
1 part vinegar
1 teaspoon liquid detergent for each 2 cups (16 fl oz) water used.
Leave to dry before walking on the carpet.

Cleaning
Sprinkle dry bicarbonate of soda (baking soda) all over the carpet, rub well in with a scrubbing brush or straw broom and leave overnight. Next day, vacuum clean. Instead of bicarbonate of soda you can use powdered magnesia or damp salt.
*Scrub a solution of ½ cup (4 fl oz) of white vinegar to 2½ cups (20 fl oz) of water into the carpet. Add more vinegar for persistant stains. Let dry and then vacuum.
*Make a solution of 4 tablespoons of bicarbonate of soda (baking soda), 6 teaspoons of household ammonia, ¼ cup (2 fl oz) of liquid detergent and 2½ cups (20 fl oz) of water. Mix well and apply with a soft brush. Wipe off excess liquid and leave to dry thoroughly. **CAUTION ▶**
*Mix some washing powder, liquid detergent and a little water and beat well with a mixer until the suds become thick and creamy and hold their shape. Apply with a soft brush in the direction of the pile. Wipe up dirty suds and finish off by going over once or twice with a clean cloth dipped in warm water and squeezed dry.

Flat Spots
Hold a steam iron as close to the carpet as possible without touching it. The steam will bring the pile up. Finally straighten pile with coarse comb or brush.

Intermittent Stain
If you have a mysterious stain on your carpet that appears in damp weather and disappears again in dry weather, it is probably caused by salt or sugar. Choose a dry day and vacuum thoroughly, then sponge area thoroughly with warm water and liquid detergent. Dry well with a cloth and when completely dry, vacuum again.

CEMENT

Bricks
Lumps of dried cement should be tapped lightly with a hammer and then scraped off with a stiff wire brush or a broken flat piece of brick.
Clean off the grey residue by scrubbing with a stiff brush dipped in a solution of one part hydrochloric acid to eight parts water, being careful not to get any on the mortar between the bricks. Leave to soak for 10 minutes. Rinse off with the hose and repeat procedure until stain is removed. **CAUTION ▶**

Tiles
Apply with an old brush, a solution of one part hydrochloric acid to eight parts water and leave to soak for 10 minutes. Rinse off with clean water. Make sure that none of the solution gets into the cement joints between the tiles. **CAUTION ▶**

CHAIR UPHOLSTERY

Padded
A dry foam rubber sponge, rubbed over the fabric will remove the loose dirt and enhance the colours. To remove grime that has accumulated over a long period, sprinkle all over with powdered magnesia and rub in well. Leave overnight, then brush off with a soft brush.

Replacing Button
Insert an ordinary hairpin through the eye in the back of the button and open the hairpin out. Bring opened ends together, push through hole in the back of the chair and let go. The hairpin will spring out and hold the button in place.

Vinyl
A regular cleaning with liquid detergent will keep material clean and to maintain the new look, rub in a little vaseline and polish off with a soft cloth.

WARNING: Do not use a solvent type cleaner on upholstery that contains foam rubber or plastic padding as the padding may be damaged.

CHERRY

Washables
Rub stain with a cut ripe tomato. Wash as usual.

CHEWING GUM

Wet well with methylated spirits, amyl acetate, kerosene, turpentine or egg white and lever off with a fairly dull steel chisel or knife. It may require repetition. **CAUTION ▶**

Clothes
See CHEWING GUM on Hair (below).

Fur
On the inside of the garment rub the gum with an ice block. When it is frozen it can be broken off.

Hair
Soak cloth in eucalyptus oil and sponge gum off.

Small Articles
Wrap in a plastic sheet and put in the freezer. When frozen just lever gum off.

CHINA

Dull
Rub well with petroleum jelly. Leave for one hour, then polish off with a clean cloth.

Stained Cracks
Dampen the cracks and then rub in baking powder. Leave for 2 hours, then wash and rinse as usual. Repeat if necessary.

CHOCOLATE

Unwashables
Sponge with methylated spirits and then use the mixture for Washables. **CAUTION ▶**

Vinyl
Clean off with hot water followed by methylated spirits.
CAUTION ▶

Washables
Soak article in a mixture of 4 tablespoons borax and 2½ cups (20 fl oz) warm water. Wash as usual.

CHROME

Cleaning
Sprinkle methylated spirits onto a clean cloth and rub over chrome. **CAUTION ▶**

Heavy Grime
Spread over the chrome a liberal amount of cutting compound, as used by automobile spray painters, and buff with a lambs' wool pad fitted to an electric drill.

Light Rust
Rub lightly but briskly with a new pad of dry fine steel wool. If necessary use a little kerosene with the steel wool. **CAUTION ▶**

Small Items
Small chrome items can be cleaned and polished at the same time by rubbing with a pencil eraser.

CIGARETTE BURNS

See BURNS, CIGARETTE (page 14).

COCKROACHES

See PEST REMOVAL (page 57).

COCONUT OIL

Place garment over blotting paper and rub well with tailors chalk. Leave for 12 hours and brush off.

COFFEE

Carpet
Mix borax with warm water and rub the area with a cloth soaked in this solution.

Cotton and Linen
Ensure first that the material will withstand boiling water.
Dab glycerine on the spot, leave for 15 minutes then spread the stained area over a saucepan or bowl and, from a height of ½ to 1 metre, pour boiling water through the cloth.
If the stain is old, spread on it a mixture of borax and water. Leave for 15 minutes and wash as usual.

Marble

First clean marble as suggested under MARBLE (page 47), using whatever method suits the surface condition of the marble, then apply the following poultice:
Mix equal quantities of hydrogen peroxide, ammonia and cream of tartar and add sufficient whiting or flour to make a paste. Spread thickly over stain and cover with plastic wrap to keep moist. Leave for 10 hours or more, then remove plastic and leave to dry. When dry, brush off and clean with liquid detergent and clean water. Repeat if necessary. **CAUTION ▶**

Unwashables

Sponge with a solution of 4 tablespoons borax to 2½ cups (20 fl oz) water followed by methylated spirits. **CAUTION ▶**

Vacuum Bottle

Make a solution of ⅓ cup (2 oz) bicarbonate of soda (baking soda) to 2½ cups (20 fl oz) water. Pour into vacuum bottle and shake well. Leave for 10 minutes. Wash as usual.

Washables

Soak in solution of 4 tablespoons borax to 2½ cups (20 fl oz) water then wash as usual.

Woollens

Mix glycerine with egg yolk and spread over the stain and leave for 30 minutes. Wash in warm water.

COLOUREDS

To enhance the colours of washables, the following are suggested:

Black

Add 1 teaspoon of brown vinegar to washing water.

Blue

Add a little salt to the washing water.

Bone/Fawn

Same as Black.

Brown

Same as Black

Cottons

Add ¼ cup (2 fl oz) brown vinegar to final rinse water.

Green

Add a small piece of alum to washing water.

Mauve

Same as Green.

Navy
Same as Black

Pink
Same as Black and add a few drops of cochineal or red ink to the final rinse water.

Red
Same as Pink.

COMPANION PLANTING

Pest Repellents
The following herbs, when growing in the garden, can assist in keeping the various insects away.

Ant: Mint, tansy.

Aphids: Chives, garlic.

Flea: Fennel, tansy.

Fruit Fly: Basil.

House Fly: Basil, chamomile, mint, rue, tansy.

Mosquito: Chamomile.

Vegetable Beetle: Oregano, wintergreen.

Vegetable Fly: Rosemary, thyme.

Vegetable Moth: Dill, hyssop, rosemary.

CONCRETE

See FLOORS, CONCRETE (page 28).

COPPER

Finger Plates, Knobs, etc.
Use ordinary brass polish.

Polishing
You can use ordinary brass polish or automobile paint cutting compound. If copper is not too dull, apply either of the above with a soft cloth. However, if badly tarnished, apply the polish with a pad of fine steel wool. Rub only in straight lines not crosswise or in circles. Finally remove polish with a soft cloth and buff to a high gleam with some cotton wool.

See TARNISH, Copper (page 71).

Pots

Mix 3 teaspoons of salt with 6 teaspoons of vinegar and rub well into copper pot with a soft cloth. Rinse in hot water and dry thoroughly.

Utensils

Cut a lemon in half, dip the cut edge in salt and rub well all over the copper utensil. Wash and rinse as usual.

WARNING: Do not use the above suggestions on simulated copper.

COSMETICS

Marble

See CREAM, Marble (page 22).

Unwashables

Sponge with eucalyptus oil.

Washables

Soak in a mixture of 1 teaspoon of ammonia to 2½ cups (20 fl oz) warm water. Wash as usual. **CAUTION ▶**

CRAYON

Paint

Rub with toothpaste and leave for 15 minutes. Wash off.

Wallpaper

Spread a sheet of blotting paper over the area and rub with a hot iron. May require repetition.

CREAM, ICE CREAM

Marble

First clean marble as suggested under MARBLE (page 47), then apply the following poultice:

Mix equal quantities of methylated spirits and acetone and add sufficient whiting or flour to make a paste. Treat the same as for *COFFEE* (page 20). **CAUTION ▶**

Unwashables

Clean with methylated spirits and when dry sponge with warm water. **CAUTION ▶**

Washables

Soak well in warm water and wash as usual.

CREASES

Listed below are various methods by which creases or pleats will be sharper and stay longer.
1. Rub a piece of damp soap on inside of crease. Iron crease on the outside using a damp cloth.
2. For dark fabric, use a cloth dipped in cold tea, placed over the crease and ironed.

Crease Resisting of Garment
Thoroughly dissolve 1 level tablespoon of gelatin in a little hot water and add to the final rinse water. Dry as normal.

Removing Stubborn Crease
Make up a solution of 5 cups (1.25 litres) warm water and 2 tablespoons of epsom salts. Mix well and soak creased garment for approximately 4 hours. Dry as normal without wringing. Finish off with a steam iron.
*Make up a solution of 5 cups (1.25 litres) warm water, 3/4 cup (6 fl oz) methylated spirits and 2 cups (16 fl oz) white vinegar. Mix well and soak creased garment for approximately 4 hours or until the crease has disappeared. Wash as usual, rinse and dry.

CURTAINS

Glazed Chintz
Wash and rinse as usual, then to retain the glazed look do as follows. To 5 cups (1.25 litres) of boiling water, add 6 tablespoons of powdered size and simmer stirring continuously till size is thoroughly dissolved. Strain well and when cool, immerse the curtains and squeeze the solution through them. To dry, let excess solution drip off, then roll up in an old towel. Do not hang on line. When nearly dry, iron curtains on the wrong side with a cool dry iron and on the right side with a fairly hot dry iron.

Lace, Nylon and Net
Because of their delicate nature, it is advisable to wash by hand in warm water and, for a crispy finish, add to the final rinse 1/2 cup (2 oz) powdered milk for white curtains or 1/2 cup (1 oz) bran for tinted curtains.
*Add 1 tablespoon of methylated spirits to the final rinse water.
CAUTION ▶

Plastic
Plastic curtains can be washed successfully in the washing machine, however if they are stained, add 6 teaspoons of a liquid bath cleaner to the washing water. Rinse by hand as spin drying will put creases in the curtains.

Plastic Shower
Add 1/4 cup (2 fl oz) kerosene to 9 litres of hot water, immerse curtains and leave for 30 minutes. Rinse in hot water and hang, full length, on clothes line to dry. **CAUTION ▶**

CUTLERY

Drying/polishing Cloth
In 2½ cups (20 fl oz) of water dissolve 2 tablespoons of whiting. Soak a tea towel in this mixture, hang to dry and use only when drying cutlery. When towel has to be washed, treat the same as above.

General Stain Remover
Three quarters fill a wide mouthed jar with water and drop in some silver paper (or ten or more milk bottle tops) and 2 teaspoons of salt. Leave jar near the sink and when required place tarnished or stained cutlery into the mixture and leave for ten minutes or more. Remove and wash and rinse as usual. Replace silver paper or milk bottle tops frequently.

Ivory or Bone Handles
Restore handles by rubbing them with a cloth dipped in hydrogen peroxide. Rinse well.
*Cut a lemon in half, dip it in salt and rub over the handles. Rinse well.
*For badly stained handles soak for 5 minutes or more in a solution of equal parts of water and bleach. Rinse well.

Silver Cutlery
To remove stains dip in damp cloth in bicarbonate of soda (baking soda) and rub well over cutlery. Wash as usual.
*Cut a potato in half and rub the raw edge over the cutlery.

See SILVER (page 66).

Stainless Steel Cutlery
To remove stains dip a damp cloth in flour and rub well over cutlery. Wash as usual.

DENTURES

Soak dentures for 30 minutes in a solution of 1 cup (8 fl oz) water and 6 teaspoons white vinegar.

DRAINS

See PIPES AND DRAINS (page 59).

DUSTING CLOTH FOR POLISHED FURNITURE

Soak a cloth in turpentine, kerosene or paraffin, wring and hang to dry. Apart from being better than an ordinary cloth it also buffs the polish and leaves the furniture more gleaming. Re-treat as necessary. **CAUTION ▶**

See FURNITURE (page 32).

DYE

Clothing

Saturate spot with lemon juice and brush in sufficient cornflour (cornstarch) to make a thick paste. When dry brush off and wash as usual.

If unsuccessful, try bleaching the whites with ordinary bleach and add a little ammonia to the rinse water. **CAUTION ▶**

Coloureds

Use hydrogen peroxide as a bleach and rinse as above.
CAUTION ▶

See HAIR RINSE (DYE) (page 37).

EGG

Carpet

Scrape off excess and lightly soak stain with a solution of 2 cups (16 fl oz) warm water, 3 teaspoons white vinegar, 6 teaspoons liquid detergent. Pat dry and if necessary repeat process.

Cutlery

Remove stains by dipping a damp cloth in coarse salt and rubbing over stains.

*Place stained cutlery in the water used to boil the eggs, leave for 10 minutes and the stain will easily wash off.

Unwashables

Spread on warm soap suds and when dry clean off with methylated spirits. **CAUTION ▶**

Washables

Wash off as much as possible in cold salted water followed when dry by an aerosol stain remover.

EMBROIDERY GUIDE LINES

Dampen a rag with methylated spirits and rub over guide lines till they disappear. Wash as usual. **CAUTION ▶**
Always test on a corner of the fabric first as some synthetics may be damaged by methylated spirits.

ENAMEL POTS, ETC.

Three quarters fill pot with water, add any acidy fruit peelings such as lemons, oranges, apples or even rhubarb and boil for 15 minutes. Pour off the boiling water and immediately pour in a little cold water. Leave for 5 minutes and then wash as usual.
*Place 4 raw and unwashed potatoes in the pot, cover potatoes with water, bring to the boil and simmer until the water has nearly evaporated. Re-cover potatoes with water, re-boil and simmer again until the water has nearly evaporated again. Repeat this procedure 4 times and then let stand overnight. Next day wash as usual.

EXHAUST FAN FILTER
METALLIC

Cleaning will be much easier if you remove most of the grease by placing the filter on some old newspaper and place in strong sunlight. Leave for a few hours until the grease melts and runs off. If further cleaning is required make up a solution of ½ cup (3 oz) caustic soda dissolved in 4.5 litres of warm water. Place filter in the solution and brush all over with an old brush. Rinse off with plenty of cold water and leave to dry. **CAUTION ▶**

FELT PEN DRIED OUT

Waterbased pen
Remove the cap at the base of the pen and pour in a few drops of water.

Waterproof Pen
Remove the cap at the base of the pen and pour in a few drops of methylated spirits. **CAUTION ▶**

FERTILIZERS

Fish Tank Water
Next time you change the water in the fish tank use it for watering indoor plants.

Milk Bottle Water
Milk bottle rinse water is a good fertilizer for maidenhair ferns.

Potato Water
Reserve the water used to boil potatoes. Allow to cool and provided it is not too salty use it to water your indoor plants. It waters and fertilizes at the same time.

Tea
Brewed tea is a good fertilizer, however use only the liquid as the leaves harden on the ground and harbour pests.

FILTER

See EXHAUST FAN FILTER, METALLIC (page 26).

FISH ODOUR

Hands
Sprinkle a little salt on your hands and rub them with a cut lemon or lemon juice.
*Wet hands and rub with a little bicarbonate of soda (baking soda).

FISH STAINS

Soak fabric with pure glycerine and leave for 4 hours. Wash as usual.

FLEAS

See PEST REMOVAL (page 57).

FLIES

See PEST REMOVAL (page 57).

FLOORS

CONCRETE

Dust Free

Coat the concrete all over with a solution of 1 cup (8 fl oz) liquid floor polish to 4 cups (1 litre) hot water. Mix well and apply with an old mop or a rag tied around a broom.

Renewing

Wash concrete with soap and water, rinse off with clean water and while still wet, sprinkle on dry cement. Leave for an hour or two then sweep clean of all cement powder. Rinse with clean water.

TERAZZO

Stains

Cut a lemon in half, dip the raw edge in salt and rub over the stain. Leave for an hour or two then rinse off with clean water.

WOODEN POLISHED

Non-slip Polish

Mix together ¾ cup (6 fl oz) boiling water, 6 teaspoons floor polish and 30 g (1 oz) piece of bar soap. Stir well to dissolve soap and when cold, add ½ cup (4 fl oz) kerosene. Add the above mixture to 5 cups (1.25 litres) of cold water and stir well. Apply to polished floor as usual and leave to dry overnight before buffing.
* To the bottle of your usual polish add ¼ cup (2 fl oz) of petrol. Apply as usual, leave to dry thoroughly and then buff well for a non-slip finish. **CAUTION ▶**

Polishing

Clean and polish at the same time by adding to 2½ cups (20 fl oz) of boiling water, 2 tablespoons of silicone type floor wax. Mix well, apply to floor as usual and when dry, rub with a soft cloth to bring up the shine.

Stains

First try removing the stains with a cloth dampened with a little turpentine. If unsuccessful, sprinkle a little turpentine on a pad of fine steel wool and rub gently over stain in direction of grain. Polish any dull spots with regular floor polish and buff well.
CAUTION ▶

FLOWERS

Prolonging the Life of Cut Flowers

The following flowers do not require any special preparation before placing in the vase. Every three days trim 6 mm (1/4 in) off the stems and replace the water.
Begonias, Camellias, Carnations, Clematis, Cosmos, Daffodils, Gardenias, Gladioli, Gypsophila (don't cut, pull out roots and all), Hyacinths, Marguerites, Narcissi, Nasturtiums, Orchids, Petunias, Snapdragons, Tulips, Verbena, Violets, Waterlilies.

The following flowers should have the bottoms of the stems scalded to a depth of 5 cm (2 in) by placing in boiling water for one minute. Every three days trim 6 mm (1/4 in) off the stems and repeat the scalding. Boiling the stems prevents them drying out.
Asters, Azaleas, Cherry Blossoms, Chrysanthemums, Dahlias, Daisies, Delphiniums, Forget-Me-Nots, Fuchsias, Hollyhocks, Hydrangeas, Iceland Poppies, Iris, Larkspurs, Marigolds, Peonies, Poinsettias, Poppies, Primrose, Roses, Ranunculi, Stocks, Sweet-Peas, Wattle, Zinnias.

The following flowers should have the bottoms of the stems crushed. Every three days, change water, cut 6 mm (1/4 in) off the stems and re-crush stem bottoms. Crushing of hard stems allows a much quicker absorption of water.
Apple Blossoms, Cherry Blossoms, Chrysanthemums, Delphiniums, Hydrangeas, Lilacs, Lilies, November Lilies, Peach Blossoms, Peonies, Roses, Stocks, Tiger Lilies.

The following flowers should have the stems split 4 cm (1 1/2 in) up from the bottom to allow a greater volume of water to be absorbed. Every three days, change the water, cut 6 mm (1/4 in) off the stems and re-split them.
Fuchsias, Lilacs, Lilies.

The following flowers will benefit by the addition of 2 tablespoons of sugar to the water in the vase.
Asters, Carnations, Cosmos, Delphiniums, Marigolds, Peonies, Petunias, Sweet-Peas.

The following flowers will benefit by the addition of 2 tablespoons of vinegar to the water in the vase.
Anemones, Gladioli, Lilies.

The following flowers will benefit by the addition of 2 tablespoons of salt to the water in the vase.
Begonias, Hollyhocks, Marguerites, Poinsettias, Roses, Snapdragons, Stocks, Violets, Wattle.

CLEANING

Plastic

Put 2 cups (10 oz) oatmeal in a paper or plastic bag, put in the flowers and seal the bag. Shake well. Leave for 10 minutes, shake again and remove the flowers.

Silk

Pour 6 teaspoons of salt in a paper or plastic bag, put in the flowers, seal the bag and shake well. Leave for 10 minutes, shake again then remove the flowers.

DRYING

Line a box with aluminium foil and pour in borax to a depth of 3-4 cm (1-1½ in). Lay flower heads on top of the borax, face down, and using a small brush, brush the borax into each petal. If the flower is intricate, pour borax all over it before turning it face down in the box. Treat each flower head in the same way, placing them next to each other in the box, but making sure that they do not touch each other. When the box is full, cover with another layer of borax at least 2.5 cm (1 in) deep. It is important to exclude all air from the flowers. For delicate flowers let stand for 24 hours, with more robust flowers taking a little longer. After 24 hours check them every 5 hours or so, because if the flowers are left too long in the borax they will fall to pieces. The borax can re-used.

FLOWER STAINS

Hands

Mix together equal parts of butter and sugar and rub well into the hands till stains disappear. Wash hands with soap and water.

FLY SPOTS

Ceiling and Walls

These may be washed off with warm water and detergent but the job will be easier if you wait for a rainy day. The dampness in the air will soften the spots.

FOOD

Unwashwable Surfaces

Sponge with a solution of 6 teaspoons liquid detergent, 2 cups (16 fl oz) warm water and 6 teaspoons of white vinegar. Pat dry and sponge with clean water.

FRAMES

Gilt

Mix equal quantities of methylated spirits and household ammonia and apply to dust-free frame with a soft, clean paint brush. Leave 10 minutes, then wipe off with a soft cloth. Do not rub too hard and do not worry if the frame is slightly sticky as it will dry out in a day or so. **CAUTION ▶**

*Warm a bottle of turpentine by placing it in a container of very hot water (not boiling), sprinkle some onto a cloth and wipe gently over the frame. Wipe off with a soft cloth. Do not worry if the frame is slightly sticky as it will dry out in a day or so.
WARNING: Turpentine is very flammable and must not be placed near or on any flame or heat source, whether electric or gas. Heat the water and pour into the container holding the bottle of turpentine away from the flame.

*Boil some onions and with a soft cloth rub the frames with the onion water. After the frame is clean, dry off with a soft cloth.

*For a really dirty frame cut a fresh onion in half and rub the raw edge over the frame. Wipe off immediately with a cloth dampened in water and finish off with a soft dry cloth.

Protect and polish gilt frames by rubbing over them with a little baby oil now and then and then polishing with a soft cloth.

FRUIT AND FRUIT JUICE

Emergency Action

As a temporary measure until you can treat the stain, sprinkle all over with salt.

Carpet

As quickly as possible absorb excess liquid, sponge stain with water and pat dry. If stain remains sponge with a solution of 2 teaspons of ammonia to 3½ cups (28 fl oz) water. Finally sponge with water and pat dry. **CAUTION ▶**

Clothes

Ensure first that fabric will withstand boiling water.
Spread stained area over a saucepan or similar and from a height of ½ to 1 metre, pour through it boiling water. When stain is removed wash as usual.
Is stain is old spread on a mixture of borax and water. Leave for 15 minutes and wash as usual.
*If washable soak in solution of 4 tablespoons borax to 2½ cups (20 fl oz) warm water. Wash as usual.
If unwashable sponge with cold water followed by glycerine.

Allow 1 hour, then sponge with lemon juice. Rinse off.
*Wet camphor block and rub over the stains. Wash as usual.

Marble

See COFFEE, Marble (page 19).

FUR

Coats

Using a firm but not too stiff brush, work in some dry, uncooked cornmeal. Let stand for 4 hours or more, then re-brush well. Shake thoroughly to remove the cornmeal and brush down with a clean brush.

Collars

Heat some bran in the oven and work well into the collar with a soft brush. When clean, shake well to remove the bran and brush with a clean brush.

Creamed White Fur Coat

Treat the same as for creamed white woollens (page 76) but do not dampen fur before applying powdered magnesia and naturally do not rinse well afterwards. Just shake well to remove the powdered magnesia. If the fur is thick, leave rolled up for at least 3 or 4 days.

FURNITURE

Antique

Mix together equal parts of linseed oil, turpentine and vinegar and rub well with a clean cloth all over the furniture. Finish with a dry cloth.
*Brown or clear shoe polish is also very good for polishing antique furniture.

Applying Polish

Furniture polish will be more effective if it is warm and applied with a damp cloth rather than a dry one. Polish off with a clean, dry pair of panty hose.
To warm polish, stand bottle in a bowl of hot water. Do not heat aerosol cans as they can explode and cause injury.
Do not polish furniture on damp days, as the moisture in the air will prevent you obtaining a high gleam.

Dusting Cloth

See DUSTING CLOTH FOR POLISHED FURNITURE (page 25).

High Gleam

To get a really high gleam on finely polished furniture such as pianos, etc. apply your usual polish and sprinkle on top a little cornflour. Rub well until all the polish is absorbed by the cornflour, leaving behind a high gleam.

Home-Made Polish

Mix equal quantities of methylated spirits, vinegar and olive oil and to every 2½ cups (20 fl oz) of this mixture add 1 tablespoon of kerosene. Mix well and shake frequently while using. Only polish small areas at a time. **CAUTION ▶**

Varnished Furniture

Test first on an inconspicuous area to ensure that the finish is really varnish and not some other type of lacquer which could be damaged.

Mix 1 tablespoon of liquid detergent with 2 tablespoons of fairly warm water and add sufficient borax to make a paste. Rub well all over the varnish and wipe off with a damp cloth. Finish off with furniture polish.

FURNITURE POLISH

Carpet

As quickly as possible absorb excess liquid. Sponge with diluted liquid detergent and then with clean water.

If any stain remains, sponge with methylated spirits followed again with detergent. Finally sponge with clean water and pat dry. **CAUTION ▶**

Clothes

Sponge stain with undiluted liquid detergent and rinse in clear water. If any stain remains, sponge with methylated spirits followed again by liquid detergent. Rinse off. **CAUTION ▶**

GENTIAN VIOLET

Soak cotton wool in a mixture of equal parts of water and *Dettol* and rub gently over the stain.

GLASS OVEN-PROOF DISHES

Sprinkle bicarbonate of soda (baking soda) over bottom of dish, cover with boiling water and leave for 10 minutes before washing as usual.

This should remove all stains, however for stubborn stains, rub with a damp cloth dipped in bicarbonate of soda (baking soda) or a piece of fine dry steel wool dipped in salt.

GLASSES STUCK TOGETHER

Immerse bottom glass, up to 3/4 of its height, in hot water. This should expand the bottom glass sufficiently to release the top glass. If the glasses are still stuck put some cold water or ice cubes into the top glass while the bottom one is still in the hot water.

GLASSWARE

Dull Glassware
Rub all over with a paste made of baking powder and water. Rinse in clean water and dry and polish with a soft cloth.
*Fill dull glassware with potato peelings and top up with water. Leave for 2 days then wash as usual.
*Fill with cold, black tea, leave for 15 minutes, then rinse with cold water and dry with a soft cloth.

Gleaming Glassware
Glassware will really sparkle if you add to the washing water some packet starch, diluted to a thin paste as per instructions on the packet.

GLOBE SHATTERED

Removal
First switch off the current and remove the jagged pieces of glass with a pair of pliers. Then press a cork bigger than the base of the globe onto the base and turn counterclockwise. The base should pop out.

GLUE

CELLULOSE

Clothes
Use nail polish remover or cellulose lacquer thinners. Soak glue stain and wash as usual. **CAUTION ▶**

LIQUID

Carpet
Lightly soak stain with a solution of 2 cups (16 fl oz) of warm water, 6 teaspoons of liquid detergent and 3 teaspoons of white vinegar. Pat dry and if necessary repeat the process.

WATER

Clothes
Warm water will usually remove water based glue. However if spots are stubborn, soak and wash in white vinegar. If unsuccessful, sponge stain with diluted acetic acid (DO NOT SATURATE FABRIC), rinse well and wash as usual.

GRASS

Sponge with methylated spirits.

Coloureds
Make a solution of glycerine and paraffin and sponge over stain. Leave for 1 hour and wash as usual.

Washables
Dampen stain with water and cover with sugar. Roll up and leave for 1 hour. Wash as usual.

Whites
Make a solution of 1 tablespoon ammonia and 2 cups (16 fl oz) water and sponge over stain. **CAUTION ▶**

GRAVY

Clothes
Treat the same as BLOOD (page 13).

GREASE

Asbestos Cement (Fibro)
Make a solution of 6 teaspoons hydrochloric acid to 2½ cups (20 fl oz) of water. Wash down using old paint brush and rinse off. **CAUTION ▶**

Carpet
Mix equal quantities of block magnesia and fullers earth with hot water. While still hot spread mixture over stain and allow to dry. Brush well and vacuum off.
* Liberally sprinkle stained area with cream of tartar or bicarbonate of soda (baking soda) and leave for 24 hours. Brush off or remove with vacuum cleaner.

Cement

See OIL, Engine (page 52).

Clothes
While grease is fresh, sprinkle with talcum powder. Leave for 30 minutes and then brush off.
If stain is stale, soak overnight in kerosene. Next day wash in very hot water with ordinary soap powder.

Cotton
Rub over spot with dry powdered starch or cornflour and press with a medium hot iron. Brush starch off and wash as usual.

Hot Grease
Throw cold water over spilt hot grease. This will set it and prevent spreading or soaking in.

Marble

See CREAM, Marble (page 22).

Overalls, Coveralls
Soak overnight in a solution of 4.5 litres of hot water and 2 tablespoons of epsom salts. Next day, wash and rinse as usual.
Instead of epsom salts, you can use either of the following: ¼ cup (2 fl oz) ammonia, ¾ cup (6 fl oz) kerosene or 1 cup (8 fl oz) vinegar. **CAUTION ▶**

Painted Woodwork
Make a solution of starch and water and paint over the stain. When dry wipe off with a soft cloth.

Paper
Place blotting paper over stain and press with a warm iron.

Polished Wood
Try rubbing lightly with kerosene. If unsuccessful make a solution of 2 teaspoons of vinegar to 1 cup (8 fl oz) of warm water. Dab on stain and remove immediately. Repeat a few times but do not let solution remain on the polished wood. Finish with a cream furniture polish. **CAUTION ▶**

Skin
Rub with cloth or cotton wool which has been soaked in baby oil.

Suede Shoes
First rub with dry oatmeal and brush off with a suede brush, then rub stains with turpentine. **CAUTION ▶**

Unwashables
Rub lightly with methylated spirits. **CAUTION ▶**

Vinyl
Scrub carefully with methylated spirits. **CAUTION ▶**

Wallpaper
Mix fullers earth and methylated spirits to a creamy paste. Spread a thick coat over wallpaper and leave for 24 hours. Wipe off. **CAUTION ▶**

* Mix talcum powder with dry cleaning fluid to a creamy consistency. Spread a thick coat over wallpaper and leave for 24 hours. Wipe off.

Walls
Wash off with turpentine. Alternatively use sugar soap. **CAUTION ▶**

Washables
Clean with eucalyptus oil and wash as usual.

GREEN STAINS

Bathtub or Sink
Soak a cloth in a solution of 2 parts household ammonia to 1 part water and hold cloth against stain. Place a weight over the cloth to hold it in place and leave for an hour or more. The green stain will now have turned blue but unlike the green stain it is washable with liquid detergent and water. Repeat if necessary. *Never use steel wool on bathtub or sink.* **CAUTION ▶**

GRILLER BROILER

Use a container large enough to hold the griller grid. The metal laundry tub is ideal. Pour in boiling water and ½ cup (3 oz) caustic soda. Mix well, immerse grid, leave to soak for 15 minutes or more and, wearing rubber gloves, scrub the grid with a wire brush or scrubbing brush. Rinse well under running water. Treatment may have to be repeated if the grease is old and caked on. **CAUTION ▶**

HAIR RINSE DYE

Carpet
Mix 1 teaspoon of methylated spirits with 4 drops of household ammonia. Rub well into stain and sponge over with carpet shampoo. **CAUTION ▶**

HANDBAGS

Leather
Use saddle soap as directed on packet.

Mesh
Sprinkle white vinegar onto a soft cloth and rub well all over the bag. Next sprinkle some ammonia onto another cloth and again

rub well all over the bag. When clean, wipe over the bag with a cloth dipped in clean water and let dry. When dry, buff well with a dry cloth.
*If only a small bag, place it in a suitable container and cover with methylated spirits. Leave for an hour or two then remove from liquid and buff dry with a soft cloth. Repeat if necessary.
CAUTION ▶

Straw (Coloured)
Treat the same as Straw (Natural) below but, instead of lemon juice use 1 tablespoon of water.

Straw (Natural)
Beat the white of 1 egg till stiff then, while beating gradually add the juice of 1 medium lemon and 1 teaspoon of epsom salts or cooking salt. Using a toothbrush, brush the mixture all over the bag, wipe over with a damp cloth to even out the coating and leave in the sun to dry.

Vinyl or Plastic
Use undiluted antiseptic such as *Dettol*. Apply with a clean cloth, rub well and dry off with a clean cloth.
*Place a little toothpaste on a damp cloth and rub lightly all over the bag. Wipe off with a dry cloth.

HANDS

General Cleaner
Add sufficient water to rolled oats to make a thick paste. Rub well all over hands and rinse off in cold water.

Rough Hands
Rub hands with vinegar and continue rubbing until vinegar dries.

HEAT MARKS

Polished Wood
Rub gently with a cloth moistened in linseed oil and use cigarette or cigar ash as a mild abrasive.
*Mix linseed oil and pumice powder into a thin paste. Rub in direction of grain and wipe off with plain linseed oil. Follow with furniture polish. Repeat if necessary.

HEM MARKS

Rub with white vinegar and leave soaking. Press with a warm iron over a cloth dampened with vinegar.

Delicates
Make a solution of 1 cup (8 fl oz) of hot water, 1 teaspoon of white vinegar and ½ teaspoon borax. Mix well, immerse ironing cloth, squeeze well. Place this cloth over the hem marks and press with a warm iron. When dry brush off any powdery deposit.

Heavy Coats, Etc.
Rub marks first with fine sandpaper before using vinegar as above.

Velvet
Use damp cloth under iron and finish off by brushing against the pile.

HOT PLATES

See STOVE/HOT PLATES (page 69).

ICE CREAM

See CREAM, ICE CREAM (page 22).

INDOOR PLANT MULCH

Coffee grounds are a good mulch for indoor plants.

See FERTILIZERS (page 27).

INK

BALL POINT

Clothes
Sponge stain with methylated spirits. When clean, wash with warm soapy water and rinse well.

Vinyl and Unwashables
Try first on an unseen part of the fabric in case it fades.
Mix equal parts of liquid bleach and methylated spirits. Add

sufficient of this mixture to fullers earth to make a paste. Rub over stains and leave until dry. Remove powder residue and rub over with a damp cloth. When dry rub in some glycerine.
CAUTION ▶
*Rub stain with eucalyptus oil.

FLUID

Bare Wood
Mix 1/4 teaspoon of oxalic acid to 3/4 cup (6 fl oz) of warm water. Apply carefully with a small brush without letting it spread. Wipe off with warm water. **CAUTION ▶**
*Sprinkle on salt and rub with lemon juice.

Carpet
While stain is fresh, cover well with dry salt. As salt absorbs the ink, brush off and replace with fresh salt. Finally sponge area with sour milk followed by methylated spirits. **CAUTION ▶**

*Saturate stained area with vinegar and mop up with sponge or blotting paper until carpet is thoroughly dry. Repeat if necessary. On light coloured carpet use white vinegar.

Clothes
Soak in a weak bleach solution for 20 minutes. Wash as usual.
* Mix mustard and spread over stain. Leave for 24 hours then sponge off with cold water and wash as usual.

Coloureds
Soak material in sour milk overnight and wash as usual. If unwashable, finish off by sponging.

Hands
First rub ink stains with vinegar and then with salt. Wash hands as usual.

Marble

See COFFEE, Marble (page 20).

Paper
Make a solution of 1 part water and 2 parts household bleach. Paint on ink and blot up immediately.

Polished Wood
Immediately absorb excess ink and treat stain with furniture polish. If stain has lightly penetrated surface try rubbing with pumice powder and a cloth dampened with linseed oil. If successful finish off with a cream furniture polish.
If unsuccessful the surface will have to be completely refinished.

Whites
Wet first, then sprinkle on salt and rub well with a slice of lemon. Leave for 1 hour. Rinse and wash as usual.

MARKING

To remove manufacturer's name, etc. from calico or sugar bags, soak in kerosene for a few hours. Wash as usual.

PRINTERS

Squeeze lemon juice through stain and rinse off. If ink is stubborn, follow by pouring through ethylene glycol or glycerine. Wash as usual.

INSECT SPRAY

Washables
Make a mixture of 1 tablespoon of borax and 2½ cups (20 fl oz) warm water. Soak overnight then wash as usual.

IODINE

Marble

See COFFEE, Marble (page 20).

IRON DRY OR STEAM

Cleaning Base
Spread toothpaste, vinegar or silver polish over the base of iron. Make sure that no toothpaste enters the steam holes. Finish off with a clean cloth dipped in methylated spirits. **CAUTION ▶**
*For non-steam irons, rub base with fine steel wool dipped in pumice powder or powdered whiting. Finish off as above.

Cleaning Hot Iron
Sprinkle salt on a clean piece of paper. Run iron over the salt, wipe clean and continue ironing.

JAM

Unwashables
Dab on warm water containing ammonia or borax. **CAUTION ▶**

Washables
Soak in a mixture of 4 tablespoons of borax to 2½ cups (20 fl oz) warm water. Wash as usual.

JEWELLERY CLEANING

Cameos
Clean with warm water and liquid detergent applied with a soft brush. Rinse and dry well.

Crystal
Make a solution of 1 teaspoon ammonia to 2½ cups (20 fl oz) hot water. If possible, immerse jewellery and leave to soak for 10 minutes. If jewellery cannot be soaked, wash with a soft cloth dipped in the above solution. Rinse in warm water and dry thoroughly. Finally dip in cologne and dry with a soft cloth.
CAUTION ▶

Diamanté
Rub gently with an impregnated silver polishing cloth.

Diamonds
Toothpaste or shaving cream applied with an old toothbrush will thoroughly clean diamonds. Rinse off in cold water and then dip in cologne and dry with a soft cloth.

Emeralds
Immerse in tepid, soapy water and rub with fingers. As emeralds are soft stones, do not use a brush. Dry with a soft cloth.

Gilt
Wash in tepid, soapy water and dry with a soft cloth.

Gold
Same as Diamanté and Diamonds.

Ivory
Sprinkle some methylated spirits onto a soft cloth and rub over ivory. Finally soak in a medium solution of household bleach for an hour or more, then rinse well and wipe dry. Sunlight helps prevent ivory from yellowing. **CAUTION ▶**

Marcasite
Same as Diamanté. Keep away from heat as this damages the sparkle of marcasite.

Pearls
Same as Gilt but do not leave to soak too long as you could damage the thread.

Pearls (Cultured)
Place pearls in small container and cover with powdered magnesia. Stir well to ensure that the pearls are thoroughly covered and leave overnight. Shake powder off and wipe with a soft cloth.

Pearls (Imitation)
Same as real pearls but handle carefully to prevent damaging the thin coating.

Rubies
Clean in tepid soapy water with a very soft brush. Dry with a soft cloth.

Sapphires
Same as Rubies

Silver

See SILVER (page 66).

Turquoise
Same as Pearls (Cultured)

JUG ELECTRIC

Three quarters fill jug with cold water, add a sliced lemon, bring to the boil and switch off. Let stand for 5 hours or so. Discard lemon slices and water and boil with fresh water once or twice to remove any traces of lemon.

JUICE

See FRUIT AND FRUIT JUICE (page 31).

KETTLES

Cast Iron and Aluminium
Three quarters fill kettle with boiling water. Add 3 teaspoons of borax or cream of tartar and let boil for approximately 15 minutes. Leave to cool, drain and remove any residue with detergent and steel wool. Wash and rinse thoroughly with boiling water. Repeat if necessary.

LACE

Crisp Finish
Dip a pressing cloth in a solution of 1 tablespoon borax to 2.5 litres of hot water. Wring out, place over lace and press with a hot iron.

Yellow
In 5 cups (1.25 litres) of cold water mix 2 teaspoons of borax. Put the lace in the solution and slowly heat but do not boil. When all the yellow has disappeared, remove from the heat, rinse well and place in the shade to dry.

LAMBSWOOL OR SHEEPSKIN

Dry Cleaning Method

Sprinkle liberally with powdered magnesia. Rub in well and roll up tightly. Wrap rolled up skin in a sheet of plastic or clean paper and leave for a week or more. Unroll skin, shake well to remove powder and finish off with a stiff clothes brush.

Wet Cleaning Method

Lightly Soiled Skins: Dissolve washing powder specifically recommended for wool in warm water and add 2 teaspoons of ammonia. Immerse skin and agitate gently for 2 or 3 minutes or until clean. Hang on line in the shade and with hose, rinse off all the soapy water.

When all the water has drained off, rub olive oil into the back of the skin and when nearly dry, work the oil into the skin by rubbing it together. When thoroughly dry, fluff the wool by brushing with a stiff clothes brush. Use care when handling wet skin as it tears easily. **CAUTION ▶**

Heavily Soiled Skins: Dissolve washing powder specifically recommended for wool in warm water and add 2 teaspoons each of ammonia, borax and glycerine. When cool rub well into the skin, doing a small area at a time and wiping up the excess dirty lather before continuing. Hang on line in the shade and with hose, rinse off all remaining dirty lather. Finish off the same as for lightly soiled skins. **CAUTION ▶**

See WOOLLENS (page 76).

LAMINATED BENCH AND TABLE TOPS

Heavy Stains

Cut a sheet of the finest grade wet and dry emery paper into handy size pieces, 10 cm x 10 cm (4 in x 4 in). Soak pieces in a soap and water solution for approximately 10 minutes then, while keeping emery paper saturated with the soap and water solution, rub all over the laminated top until stains are removed. To restore the high gloss dulled by the emery paper see Polishing below.

Light Stains

Rub well with a rag dipped in olive oil or lemon juice.

Moderate Stains

Make a thick paste of bicarbonate of soda (baking soda) and water and rub well into stain. Leave paste on 2 hours or more, then wipe off. Repeat if necessary.

Polishing

After washing and drying laminated top, rub in a thin coat of silicon car polish. When dry, polish well and apply another thin coat of polish. Again when dry, polish well. This should result in a really high gloss. However, if not satisfied repeat procedure.

LAMPSHADES

Parchment

To 2½ cups (20 fl oz) of warm water add 1 teaspoon liquid detergent and 2 teaspoons of methylated spirits. Mix well and rub gently over shade with a damp sponge. Wipe off with a sponge dipped in clean water and place shade on lamp to dry. For quicker drying, switch on the lamp. When dry, apply a thin starch solution with a sponge. This will keep the shade clean much longer and make cleaning easier next time. **CAUTION ▶**

Plastic

Sprinkle liquid antiseptic, such as *Dettol*, onto a clean cloth and wipe over the shade. Wipe dry with a clean cloth.

LEATHER

Cleaning

A good general cleaner for leather is saddle soap which you can buy from hardware stores or saddlery shops. Rub soap in well with a damp sponge and when leather is clean dry off with a soft cloth.

* Petroleum jelly
* One tablespoon of vinegar and 1 tablespoon ammonia diluted with 3¾ cups (30 fl oz) warm water. **CAUTION ▶**
* Eucalyptus oil
* Half a teaspoon of borax mixed with 2½ cups (20 fl oz) of warm water.

Apply any of the above with a clean cloth or sponge.

Do's and Don'ts

Never use hot water on leather as it could distort and shrink.
Never use furniture polish, waxes, paraffin oil, shellac or varnish.
Do not saturate leather with water.
When cleaning or polishing rub fairly briskly but not hard.
Clean leather at least once a month and do not let dust accumulate.

Restoring

After cleaning, rub briskly all over with a cloth dipped in raw linseed oil, glycerine or castor oil. Rub in one direction only to avoid streaking.

LINEN

Yellowed
Boil linen in a little water in which is placed a cheese cloth containing crushed egg shells. When linen is white, remove from boiling water and wash as usual.

LINOLEUM OR VINYL

Maintenance
Mix together equal quantities of kerosene, methylated spirits and household ammonia. Immerse a large cloth in the above solution, leave to soak for 5 minutes then, without wringing, hang on the line in the shade to dry thoroughly. To use, rub over polished linoleum floor everyday or so. **CAUTION ▶**

Polish
Raw linseed oil rubbed over linoleum, left for 30 minutes, then wiped dry, will make linoleum really gleam.

Removing Layers of Polish
Sprinkle turpentine all over linoleum and rub well with a rag or an old mop. Clean off the turpentine and old polish with hot water. **CAUTION ▶**

Removing Stains
Sprinkle a little kerosene on a pad of fine steel wool and rub over the stains. Clean kerosene off with warm water and liquid detergent. **CAUTION ▶**

LIPSTICK

Rub lightly with white vinegar or eucalyptus oil on a moistened cloth.

Washables
Rub glycerine into stain and leave for 30 minutes. Sprinkle soap powder or ammonia on stain and wash as usual. **CAUTION ▶**

MARBLE

Cleaning and Re-juvenating
Mix together the following:
1 part fine pumice powder
2 parts washing soda
1 part fine powdered chalk
1 part white vinegar
Sufficient water to make a paste.
Rub the above mixture all over the marble with a soft cloth and when clean, wash off with liquid detergent and water.
Any small imperfections can be sanded off with fine wet and dry emery paper. Soak paper in water for 10 minutes, wrap around a cork sanding block and rub gently in the direction of the grain only. Keep immersing the paper in water to prevent build up of marble dust.

Heavy Surface Dirt and Grime
Make a solution of 1 part hydrochloric acid to 5 parts water and apply to marble with an old brush. Leave to soak for 15 minutes, then rinse off with clean water. **CAUTION ▶**

Light Surface Dirt and Grime
Sprinkle turpentine onto a clean cloth and wipe well all over the marble. Wash off with warm water and detergent and if still not quite clean, rub gently with scouring powder and water. Wash off with clean water. **CAUTION ▶**

Polishing
First clean marble as suggested above, then with a soft cloth, dipped in a combination of cutting and polishing compounds as used for automotive paintwork, rub the marble in one direction of the grain only. Leave until dry, then buff well and finally apply a silicone based liquid floor wax. Polish well.

MEDICINES

Dilute stain with a little warm water and sponge with diluted detergent. Pat dry. If unsuccessful, consult the pharmacist.

MENDING INVISIBLE

Small tears can be quickly repaired by applying a little clear nail polish to both sides of the tear and holding the sides together until stuck. If this method is used carefully, the repair will be virtually invisible and will stand up to washing.
For larger tears or small holes, cut a matching piece of material slightly larger than the tear or hole from the inside of a seam or

cuff and cut a similar size piece of polythene plastic material or iron-on tape. Turn the garment inside out, place the piece of plastic on the tear and place the matching material on top of the plastic. With a very hot iron press the patch until the plastic melts and holds the material in place. Finally apply a little clear nail polish around the edges of the hole to stop any tendency to lift. Wash normally.

*Cut a slightly oversize patch of matching material. Turn the garment inside out, place on a flat surface and saturate material around the hole with egg white. Apply patch over hole and press firmly until the egg white is dry. Smooth out any wrinkles with a warm iron. Wash as usual.

MICE

See PEST REMOVAL (page 57).

MILDEW

Books

Immerse a cheese cloth or similar in a solution of 6 teaspoons of copper sulphate and 2½ cups (20 fl oz) water. Saturate well, wring and hang on a line to dry. When completely dry rub over books thoroughly.

This method will not damage the books and the cloth can treat approximately fifty books before it requires re-treatment.

CAUTION ▶

Brick or Stone

First remove loose mould with a wire brush. Mix 5 litres of water and 3 tablespoons copper sulphate together and rub well over mould. Repeat until mould is removed. Sometimes after this treatment a bluish bloom is evident. This will fade when exposed to rain. When completely dry, surface may be painted.

CAUTION ▶

China

If mildew is very deep and on old delicate china it is best to get the experts to treat it. However if mildew is not too deep, rub petroleum jelly over stain and leave in a cool oven overnight. Next day wash and make sure the china is thoroughly dry as mildew can only grow in wet conditions.

Holland Blinds

Rub the stain well with damp salt. When dry brush off and wipe over with damp cloth.

Leather
Rub well all over the stain with a liberal amount of vaseline or petroleum jelly. Leave for 1 hour and then wipe dry.
*Mix one part hydrochloric acid with eight parts of water and using an old paint brush, brush over mildew and hose off. **CAUTION ▶**

Leather Books
Sprinkle a little household ammonia onto a clean cloth and wipe mould away. **CAUTION ▶**

Mildew Remover
Mix the following:
125 g (4 oz) white starch
1/2 cup (4 fl oz) lemon juice
125 g (4 oz) soft soap (from pharmacist)
1/4 cup (2 oz) common salt
Apply to stain and leave in open air for 2 hours. Wash and rinse well.

Washables (Coloureds)
Soak in sour milk and let dry in the sun.

Washables (Whites)
If mildew is fresh, just wash in soap and water. If it is an old stain, squeeze lemon juice onto the stain followed by salt. Leave in the sun to dry then wash as usual.

MILK

Cement
Spread wet sand over the stain. With a flat sandstone block rub stain until it disappears. If stubborn, a little hydrated lime mixed with the sand will help. Do not use ordinary soap powders.

Marble
See CREAM, Marble (page 22).

Polished Wood
Wipe up excess milk and treat with furniture polish. If still stained treat as for ALCOHOL, Spirits (page 8).

Unwashables
Sponge with methylated spirits and when dry, clean with warm water.

Washables
Soak in warm water and wash as usual. If stubborn, sprinkle on borax and soap powder and pour hot water through the stain. Rub gently, leave for 10 minutes and then wash as usual.

MOHAIR

Mohair will retain its softness if you add 4 tablespoons of baby shampoo to the washing water. If using the washing machine, turn the garment inside out to minimise damage.

MOSQUITOES

See PEST REMOVAL, (page 57).

MOTHS

See PEST REMOVAL, (page 57).

MUD DRY

Heavy Fabric
Rub with raw potato.

Light Fabric
Wash in ammonia and water and rinse well. **CAUTION ▶**

MULBERRY

Hands
Rub well with green mulberries and wash with warm water.

NAIL POLISH

Clothes
Carefully so as not to spread the stain, sponge with non-oily nail polish remover such as acetone. Clean remaining smear with methylated spirits and pat dry.
If stain is persistent apply a few drops of chemically pure amyl acetate. Let soak for a few minutes and pat dry. **CAUTION ▶**

WARNING: Some synthetic materials may be damaged by polish remover. Test on a seam for suitability.

Polished Wood
Mix equal quantities of vinegar and olive oil and rub on nail polish with a cloth dipped in warm water. May require repeated

rubbing. When stain has been removed restore surface of polished wood by polishing with a mixture of equal parts of linseed oil and turpentine. **CAUTION ▶**

Prevent Chipping
Nail polish will stick better if you dip your nails into vinegar before applying the polish. Do not wipe off the vinegar but allow it to dry naturally.

Quick Drying Nail Polish
After applying polish, dip fingers in icy cold water for approximately 2 minutes. Polish will dry very quickly.

NAILS BREAKING

Reduce the tendency for nails to break by rubbing nails with pure honey. Leave for 10 minutes and wash off.

NICOTINE

Fingers
Rub with nail polish remover.

NON-STICK PANS

You can buy special nylon pads for cleaning non-stick pans, however a piece of nylon netting crumpled up into a ball and used with detergent will also do the job.
For badly caked-on food, sprinkle bicarbonate of soda (baking soda) over bottom of pan and cover lightly with bleach. Leave to soak for 5 minutes then add a little water and let boil for 10 minutes. Wash as usual.

NYLON AND RAYON

Sewing
Stop nylon slipping and improve machine feeding by rubbing wet soap along where you are going to sew. Let dry before sewing.

Whiten and Deodorise
Add 6 teaspoons of methylated spirits to both the washing and rinse water. **CAUTION ▶**
⋆Soak garment in cold or warm water to which is added either 4 tablespoons bicarbonate of soda (baking soda) or borax.

OIL

Blankets
Mix 1 tablespoon borax and 1 tablespoon soft soap in 10 litres of water. Soak blankets for 24 hours. Rinse well and hang to dry without wringing.
CAUTION ▶ Use only plastic, glass or porcelain enamel container to soak blankets.

Bricks
Add enough whiting to methylated spirits to make a thick paste. Saturate oil stain with pure methylated spirits, then apply a liberal amount of the thick paste and leave to dry. When dry, brush off the dried paste and wash off any remaining white residue with clean water and a stiff brush. Repeat if necessary. **CAUTION ▶**

Carpets
Liberally sprinkle stained area with cream of tartar and leave for 24 hours. Brush off or remove with vacuum cleaner.

Clothes
While stain is still fresh sprinkle on talcum powder. Leave for 30 minutes and brush off.

Clothes (Old Stains)
Work from the outer edge of the stain and rub in glycerine and leave to soak for 1 hour. Sponge off with a solution of warm water and detergent.

Marble

See CREAM, Marble (page 22).

Shoes
Cleaning fluids will remove oil stains, but they also remove some of the colouring and leave an obvious spot. Instead of fluids, dab rubber cement on the stain and smooth it down with your finger. When dry, rub off the rubber cement. This may have to be repeated a number of times but there will be no spot left behind.

ENGINE

Cement
If oil is fresh sprinkle a liberal amount of dry cement over it and brush in well. As cement absorbs the oil, replace with fresh cement and continue until the stain is absorbed.
If stain is dry, mix some caustic soda with very hot water and brush well all over the stain. Leave to soak for 30 minutes and wash off. Follow with the treatment of dry cement as suggested above. **CAUTION ▶**

Clothes
If stain is fresh, sprinkle on talcum powder. Leave for 30 minutes and brush off. If stain is old, soak overnight in kerosene. Next day, wash in very hot water with your usual soap powder.
CAUTION ▶

LINSEED

Linseed oil, if left on too long may become sticky and difficult to remove. However, a cloth sprinkled with a little kerosene and rubbed over the sticky surface will assist in removing it.
CAUTION ▶

ONION ODOUR

Add 1 teaspoon of vinegar to the washing up water.

OVEN

Clean
While oven is warm, place inside a cloth saturated with household ammonia and close the door. When cool the grease will wipe off. If you do this once a week your oven will always stay clean.
CAUTION ▶

Door Glass
Sprinkle bicarbonate of soda (baking soda) onto a wet sponge and rub well all over the glass.

PAINT

ENAMEL

Carpet
Dab paint spot with mineral turpentine to soften. Peel paint off and sponge with a solution of 1 teaspoon of detergent, 1 teaspoon of white vinegar and 1 litre of warm water. Pat dry.
CAUTION ▶

Cement
Make a solution of 1 cup (6 oz) caustic soda to 2½ cups (20 fl oz) of hot water. Spread on paint spots and allow to soak for about 5 hours. Wash off. Repeat if necessary. **CAUTION ▶**

Lino and Vinyl
Using hot water, dissolve starch into a paste and apply to the paint spot while hot. Leave for 30 minutes and wipe off.

Skin (Child's)
As kerosene or turpentine may be too harsh for a child's skin, saturate a piece of cotton wool with baby oil and gently rub over the paint spots. Wash off.

Slate
Paint on a liberal amount of paint remover and to prevent evaporation cover with wet paper or dry blotting paper. Leave for 30 minutes then scrape off with a wire brush. Finally clean with

kerosene. If unsuccessful apply a solution of 6 teaspoons of hydrochloric acid to 2 cups (16 fl oz) of water then wash off. **CAUTION ▶**
If still unsuccessful grind paint spots off with a carborundum stone.

Steel
Use paint thinners. **CAUTION ▶**

Textured Bricks
Apply a proprietary brand of paint remover with an old paint brush. Wait approximately 5 minutes and then scrape off with a wire brush. Repeat if necessary.

Washables
Soften with glycerine then make a solution of equal parts of turpentine and ammonia and sponge over the stain. Wash as usual. **CAUTION ▶**

Wooden Floor
Mix together ¼ cup (2 fl oz) turpentine with ½ cup (4 fl oz) ammonia and place on paint spots to soften. Dip a piece of steel wool into the mixture and rub softened paint spots until they disappear. **CAUTION ▶**

ODOUR
Place a bucket of cold water containing 3 chopped onions in the centre of the room for a few hours.

PAVING
Washables
Rub well on front and back of paint spot with cold cream. Do this for approximately 10 minutes with continual replenishment of the cream, then spread a thick layer over the spot and leave for 24 hours. Wash as usual.

PLASTIC
Clothes
Soak and then rub gently with toothbrush in a mixture of salt and hot water. If paint is too hard, soak first in methylated spirits followed by above salt and water treatment. **CAUTION ▶**

PAINTWORK

Home Made Cleaner
Make up a solution of 6 teaspoons methylated spirits to 2.5 litres of water and sponge over the paintwork. Test on an inconspicuous area and, if too severe, increase the amount of water. **CAUTION ▶**
*Mix equal quantities of ammonia and warm water and sponge over the paintwork. **CAUTION ▶**

PASPALUM GUM

Apply eucalyptus extract with a brush. When dry wipe off with a stiff brush.

PASTE

Wallpaper
If paste has stuck to the front of the wallpaper, remove by placing on it a sponge dipped in warm water. Repeat two ~~or~~ three times after which the softened paste should come off by rubbing gently with a dry cloth.

PASTRY CUTTER

Remove the serrated metal strip from an aluminium foil dispenser box, or similar. Form into the shape desired and fasten the ends with sticky tape.

PENCIL INDELIBLE

Cotton or Linen
Rub back and front of stain with butter. After 30 minutes soap well and wash in warm soapy water. Rinse well. If still stained, rub with methylated spirits. **CAUTION ▶**

Wood
Make a mixture of lemon juice and salt and rub well into the stain. Leave for 5 or 10 minutes to dry and wash off.

PERFUME

Clothes
Rub well with glycerine and wash as usual.

Wood or Lacquer
Dampen tissue paper with acetone or nail polish remover and gently rub surface. Keep the tissue moving as damage may occur if left in the one spot. **CAUTION ▶**

PERSPIRATION

Odour
Dissolve 2 non-coloured aspirin powders in water and sponge over area. Hang to dry.
*Sponge area with lemon juice or white vinegar diluted with a little water and hang to dry.
*On synthetic materials sponge area with a solution of 2½ cups (20 fl oz) of cold water and 4 tablespoons bicarbonate of soda (baking soda).

Shirts
Soak shirts in a strong solution of glauber salts and water. Then fill separate tub with warm water, add cloudy ammonia and soak shirts for 30 minutes. Wash as usual and dry in the sun. If stain is still evident, rub on lemon juice, leave for 30 minutes, rinse off in warm water and allow to dry in the sun. **CAUTION ▶**
*Sponge stain with hydrogen peroxide and leave in the sun for about 1 hour.

Unwashables
Sponge with a weak solution of methylated spirits.
CAUTION ▶

Washables
Sponge with a weak solution of white vinegar or ammonia and wash as usual. **CAUTION ▶**

Woollens
Mix 2 teaspoons of borax with 1¼ cups (10 fl oz) of warm water and sponge over the stain.

PEST EXTERMINATION CARDS

Add a little water to 1 cup (4 oz) plain (all-purpose) flour and mix to a smooth paste. Add 2 tablespoons of powdered sodium fluosilicate, 1 tablespoon of powdered gelatin, ⅔ cup (5 oz) of sugar, ¾ teaspoon of salt and 6¼ cups (1.75 litres) of cold water. Mix well, then slowly heat stirring continuously to a smooth paste.
Cut pieces of cardboard, approximately 10 cm x 10 cm (4 in x 4 in) and spread the paste on both sides of the cardboard. Hang to dry. When dry suspend with string in your wardrobe or place wherever necessary. These cards will keep killing moths for over 2 years.

PEST REMOVAL

Ants

Sprinkle borax on shelves. Place slices of lemon, fresh or stale, along the paths travelled by ants. Rub kerosene on woodwork around windows, doors and skirting boards. Paint the inside of kitchen cupboards with a solution of 3 teaspoons of alum dissolved in 2 cups (16 fl oz) of hot water. **CAUTION ▶**

* Sprinkle infested areas with liberal amounts of pepper or spray area with liquid chlordane.

Cockroaches

Make up a mixture of 3 parts boracic acid, 3 parts sodium fluoride, 1 part icing sugar and 2 parts cocoa.

Put the mixture in areas frequented by cockroaches such as hot water heaters, under the kitchen sink, dark storage areas, etc. Replace mixture as required.

Paint inside of kitchen cupboards with a solution of 3 teaspoons alum dissolved in 2 cups (16 fl oz) of hot water.

Fleas

Sprinkle carpets and floors with a liberal amount of cooking salt Leave for 10 minutes and then remove with vacuum cleaner.

Flies

Rub on skin a few drops of oil of lavender.

Rub face with petroleum jelly to which a few drops of oil of citronella have been added.

* Rub skin with a mixture of 2 tablespoons epsom salts to 2 cups (16 fl oz) water.
* Sprinkle the inside of the garbage bin with powdered borax.
* Rub paraffin oil or ammonia on framework around windows and doors.
* Fresh mint on the table or in a vase near a window will usually keep flies away.
* A sponge dipped in boiling water and then sprinkled with a few drops of oil of lavender and left in the middle of a room will also keep flies away. Replenish water once or twice a day and lavender every 4 days.
* Heat some cloves in the oven for approximately 15 minutes and place in a saucer near an open window.

Mice

Setting Trap

Always wear rubber gloves when setting a mouse trap to avoid the smell of a human being left on the trap.

Cleaning Trap

After catching a mouse, wash trap in soap and water and rinse well to get rid of the smell of the dead mouse.

Baits

A pumpkin seed appears to be very attractive to mice.

A plump raisin also works well.

A piece of bread crust flavoured with vanilla is usually successful.

Mosquitoes

Rub on skin a few drops of oil of lavender.
Rub on face some petroleum jelly to which a few drops of oil of citronella have been added.
A planter containing basil placed near an open window is very effective in deterring mosquitoes.

Moths

Sprinkle a few drops of ammonia onto a piece of cloth and leave in your wardrobe. Brush cracks, joints and crevices in furniture, wardrobes and cupboards with 3 teaspoons of alum dissolved in 2 cups (16 fl oz) of hot water. **CAUTION ▶**

Silverfish

Treat the same as for Ants or Moths.

PEWTER

Cleaning and Polishing

Make a paste of whiting mixed with a little linseed oil and rub well into the pewter. When stains are removed, wash with soap and water (not detergent), and polish dry with a soft cloth.
To prevent stains recurring, wash with soap and water every 3 or 4 weeks.

PHOTOGRAPHS

Sprinkle a few drops of methylated spirits onto a clean, soft cloth and gently rub over dirty photographs.
CAUTION ▶

PIANO

Keys
Try one of the following methods to clean piano keys and whiten them.
1. Add sufficient hydrogen peroxide, methylated spirits or lemon juice to some whiting to make a paste and rub well over the keys. Leave for 1 hour or so, then wipe off and rub keys with undiluted hydrogen peroxide. **CAUTION ▶**
2. Saturate a soft cloth with methylated spirits or eau-de-cologne, dip in some talcum powder or powdered milk and rub well over the keys. **CAUTION ▶**
3. If the discolouration of the keys is really bad, the best thing you can do is to remove them, one by one, and rub them with very fine wet or dry emery paper. Let the emery paper soak in water for 10 minutes or more, wrap it around a cork rubbing block and rub each key gently in direction of grain only. Dip the emery paper and cork in water frequently. When clean, wipe each key dry, replace in piano and apply some liquid floor polish. Buff well.

Musty
Make a small bag out of netting, fill with mothballs and hang inside the piano.

PIPES AND DRAINS

Kitchen or Laundry Sink
Pour down the sink, a solution of 5 tablespoons borax to 2½ cups (20 fl oz) boiling water.
* Pour down the sink a strong brew of black coffee.
* Pour down the sink every week, hot salted water.

PLASTIC

Machine Sewing
Place waxed paper along where you are going to sew. Attach to plastic with sticky tape and when sewing is finished rip off the paper.

POTS, PANS, DISHES

See BURNS – POTS, PANS, DISHES (page 14).
See NON-STICK PANS (page 51).

PLAYING CARDS

See CARDS, PLAYING (page 16).

PRE-WASH STAIN REMOVER

Mix together the following:
1 1/4 cups (10 fl oz) hydrogen peroxide
1 cup (8 fl oz) methylated spirits
5 tablespoons cloudy ammonia
1/4 cup (2 fl oz) pure glycerine

Store in a well sealed bottle and apply to stains 30 minutes before washing. Wash as usual. **CAUTION ▶**
*Moisten the stained area with cold water and sprinkle on a little sugar. Leave overnight and next day wash as usual.

PRICE TAGS & LABELS

Stick-on price tags cannot always be removed cleanly. However, a drop or two of kerosene or eucalyptus oil on a rag and rubbed on lightly will remove the residue. **CAUTION ▶**

PRINT BLACK

Sugar or Flour Bags
Saturate printing with kerosene and leave for 30 minutes. Mix some washing powder with cold water and let bag soak for at least 24 hours. Finally rub printed area well and rinse thoroughly in cold water. Hang to dry. Repeat if necessary. **CAUTION ▶**

RAINCOATS

To 2 1/2 cups (20 fl oz) warm water add 6 teaspoons of ammonia. Sponge over the stained area and hang to dry. **CAUTION ▶**
*Cut a raw potato in half and rub over stains.
*If the raincoat is made of gaberdine, heat salt in the oven and rub over the stains.

RAYON

See NYLON AND RAYON (page 51).

REFRIGERATOR

Odour

Cut a lemon in quarters and squeeze the juice from 3 pieces into a bowl of water. Place the remaining piece unsqueezed in the water. Leave the bowl in the refrigerator and renew each week.
*Leave in the refrigerator an open bottle of vanilla essence or a cut lemon.

RUBBER HEEL MARKS

Squeeze toothpaste on a soft cloth and rub over marks.

RUGS

Afghan

Lay rug on a flat surface and soak with a solution of *2 1/2 cups (20 fl oz) of cold water, 2 1/2 cups (20 fl oz) of white vinegar, 3 cups (24 fl oz) of methylated spirits and 1/3 cup (3 oz) of salt.*
Brush on gently with a soft brush, stretch into shape and place clean weights all around. When dry, remove weights and lightly brush with a soft dry brush. **CAUTION ▶**

Cashmere and Llama

Wash as you would a woollen garment. Use only the special washing powder made for woollen garments and use only warm water to wash and rinse.

RUST

Bath

Mix to a paste bicarbonate of soda (baking soda), lemon juice and salt and rub over rust stains. Wash off.
*Mix hydrogen peroxide and cream of tartar to a creamy paste. Spread on stains and leave for 10 minutes, then rub lightly and wash off. Clean as usual.

Ceramic Tiles
Mix ½ cup (5 oz) of commercial glycerine and 2 tablespoons of sodium citrate with sufficient water to make a thin solution. Add whiting till creamy. Apply liberally over stain and leave for at least 6 hours. Wash off.

Cotton and Linen
Wet stains thoroughly with water and dab on small amount of hydrochloric acid. Wash in warm soapy water. **CAUTION ▶**

Enamel Surfaces
Mix the following to a fairly thick paste:
4 tablespoons vinegar
4 tablespoons flour
8 tablespoons hydrogen peroxide
Spread over stain and leave for a few hours. Wash off with cold water.

Marble
First clean marble as suggested for FRUIT STAINS (page 31), then apply the following poultice: Add sufficient whiting or flour to a commercial rust reducing chemical to make a paste. Let dry and wipe off.

Nickel
Coat with petroleum jelly and leave for 4 days. Clean off with cloth dipped in ammonia. **CAUTION ▶**

Paper
This is a result of ageing and there is nothing you can do about it.

Polished Metal
Scrape off with copper scraper rather than with abrasive paper or steel knife. The copper will not scratch.

Scissors
Dip a piece of fine steel wool in kerosene and rub over scissors until rust is removed. Prevent further rusting by rubbing with a little salad oil if they are kitchen scissors or mineral oil on other scissors. Remove oil before next using the scissors.
CAUTION ▶

Sinks
Cut a lemon in half, dip the raw edge in salt and rub over the stains. Rinse off immediately with clean water.
*Sprinkle vinegar onto cloth and rub over stain. Rinse off immediately with clean water.

Steel Knives
Remove most of the rust with steel wool and finish off by rubbing both sides of the knife with a cut, raw onion. Leave knife covered in onion juice for approximately 1 hour. Wash well and re-sharpen.

Tin (Pots, pans and dishes)
Mix one part hydrochloric acid with 6 parts water and pour into rusty dish. Leave for 3 minutes then discard acid. (If pouring

acid into the sink, have the cold water running to avoid damage.) Clean dish as usual, rinse well and dry thoroughly.

CAUTION ▶

*If rust is very light, just rub with a damp cloth dipped in bicarbonate of soda (baking soda).

*Cut an onion in half and rub the raw edge over the rust. Leave for 20 minutes and if necessary, repeat. Wash and dry as usual but before putting away, rub again with a raw onion to prevent rust recurring.

Tools

Mix *1 tablespoon of ammonium citrate in 2½ cups (20 fl oz) water.* Soak tools for 24 hours then rinse and smear with oil.

Washables

Mix equal portions of cream of tartar and salt. Wet material and rub in well. Leave in the sun to dry. Wash as usual.

*If the stain is stubborn, boil the fabric in a mixture of 2½ cups (20 fl oz) water and 2 teaspoons of cream of tartar. Rinse well.

Woollens

Squeeze lemon juice over stain and cover with salt. When dry brush off. May require repetition. Wash as usual.

SALT WATER

Clothes

Remove encrusted salt and wash as usual but add to the washing water 6 teaspoons white vinegar for every 2½ cups (20 fl oz) of water.

SCORCH MARKS

Carpet (Light Coloured)

Make the following solution:

1¼ cups (10 fl oz) household bleach
5 tablespoons lemon juice
1 cup (8 fl oz) water

Sponge the solution over the scorch mark and repeat until the mark fades.

Coloureds

Dampen scorch mark and rub some cornflour in well. Leave to dry and iron as usual.

Nylon, Wool or Mohair

Sponge with diluted peroxide (1 part hydrogen peroxide to 4 parts water) and wash in warm soapy water with a little added borax. Ensure that all borax is rinsed off.

SCORCH MARKS cont.

Unwashables
Make a solution of 1 teaspoon borax to 1¼ cups (10 fl oz) hot water and spread over mark. Sponge off with clean water.

Whites
Wet area with diluted hydrogen peroxide (1 part hydrogen peroxide to 4 parts water) and place in sunlight. May need repetition.
* Soak a cloth in diluted hydrogen peroxide (1:4) and place over scorch mark. Cover with a dry cloth and press with a medium hot iron. At no time allow iron to come in direct contact with cloth soaked in hydrogen peroxide or dampened fabric as it may cause rust stains.

SCRATCHES

Furniture
Make a solution of 1 part white vinegar to 2 parts olive oil and rub well into the scratch. On dark furniture use brown vinegar.

SEDIMENT

Decanters and Glasses
Add 1 tablespoon of salt to 1 cup (8 fl oz) of vinegar and pour into the decanter or glass. Shake well and leave overnight giving an occasional shake. Next day, wash and rinse as usual.
* Add a tablespoon of household ammonia to 2 cups (16 fl oz) water and treat as above. **CAUTION ▶**

SHARPENING SCISSORS

Cut some fine sand paper or wet and dry paper into thin strips with the scissors. The cutting action sharpens the scissors. If sand paper isn't available, try cutting some fine steel wool pads in halves.

SHEEPSKIN

See LAMBSWOOL OR SHEEPSKIN (page 44).

SHELLS

Polishing

Rub well with a new pad of fine dry steel wool. If the shell is very rough, use a little brass polish and for a high gleam, finish off with a dry pad.
If the shell is heavily encrusted with sea life, brush on a solution of equal parts of hydrochloric acid and water. Wash off solution frequently and re-apply until cleaned. Do not leave solution on too long as the shell could be damaged. **CAUTION ▶**
When clean proceed to polish as above.
To protect final finish, paint with 1 coat of clear shellac.

SHOE POLISH

Clothes

Scrape off excess polish and sponge stain with undiluted liquid detergent. Rinse in clean water and if any stain remains, sponge with methylated spirits followed again by liquid detergent as above. Rinse off. **CAUTION ▶**

Soften

To soften shoe polish, add 3 or 4 drops of kerosene or turpentine and place tin in a warm oven for 10 minutes or so. To keep it soft add 3 or 4 drops of castor oil and mix well. **CAUTION ▶**

SHOES

Linen

Rub with a cloth dipped in white vinegar.

Suede

Cleaning: Dip a clean cloth in white vinegar and rub gently all over each shoe. When dry, brush well with an old pair of panty hose.
Bruised or Shiny: Apply a very thin coating of talcum powder and rub very gently in a circular motion with either very fine sandpaper or steel wool. Next, remove any remaining talcum powder by going over the shoe with sticky tape wrapped around your fingers, sticky side out. Finally, brush well with an old pair of panty hose.
Brushing: Instead of a suede brush, use an old pair of panty hose.
Dusty: Remove the dust by pressing sticky tape over each shoe. Replace sticky tape as required.

Tennis

Shaving cream worked into a lather and applied to tennis shoes with an old shaving brush makes a very good cleaner. Leave until dry and brush off.

White

Use undiluted antiseptic such as *Dettol*. Apply with a clean cloth, rub well and dry off with a clean cloth.
*Place a little toothpaste on a damp cloth and rub lightly all over shoe. Wipe off with dry cloth.

SHOWER ROSE

To clean accumulated deposits of lime, unscrew shower rose from the wall and soak overnight in vinegar. Next day, while still in the vinegar, brush with an old toothbrush, rinse well in clean water and re-fit.

SHOWER SCREENS
GLASS

Dip a soap filled pad of fine steel wool into vinegar and rub away all accumulated scum and soap. Rinse off with clean water.
*A cloth, dampened with methylated spirits, will also remove the scum and soap. **CAUTION ▶**

SILK

Wash only in warm soapy water and rinse in warm water to which is added 1 teaspoon of methylated spirits. Dry on netting stretched across 2 clothes lines. The methylated spirits enhances the colour and helps restore the silk sheen when ironed. Wash only by hand. **CAUTION ▶**

SILVER

Badly Tarnished

Rub tarnished silver with a cloth dipped in ammonia and whiting. Rinse off in boiling water. Finally clean with methylated spirits and rub thoroughly dry. **CAUTION ▶**

Badly Tarnished Small Items

To *2½ cups (20 fl oz) of warm water add 1 teaspoon of salt and 2 teaspoons bicarbonate of soda (baking soda).* Mix well, immerse silver items and leave until tarnish disappears. Wash in warm water and detergent and rub thoroughly dry.

Cutlery

See SILVER CUTLERY (page 24).

Jewellery

Rub silver jewellery with toothpaste using a soft brush. Rinse off in warm water and dry thoroughly.

Polishing Cloth

Maintain the gleam on silver by making your own polishing cloth as follows:
Mix together *2 tablespoons of household ammonia, 3 teaspoons of plate powder and 2 cups (16 fl oz) of warm water.*
Soak a flannelette cloth in the above mixture overnight. Next day, hang outside in the shade to drip dry – do not wring.
Rub the silver with this cloth every now and then and it will always be shiny. **CAUTION ▶**
* Soak a flannelette cloth in milk for 30 minutes then slowly bring the milk, together with the cloth, to the boil. Hang outside in the shade to dry without wringing. Use as above.

Storing

Prevent tarnishing by first cleaning with powdered starch and then placing in a storage container with 3 or 4 pieces of camphor, chalk or a satchel of silica-gel.

Stubborn Stains

On solid silver (not silver plate) most stubborn stains can be removed by rubbing with a typewriter eraser.

SILVERFISH

See PEST REMOVAL (page 57).

SLIPPERS

Felt

Clean felt or material type slippers with carpet shampoo. Mix a little shampoo according to the directions and apply to slippers with a nailbrush or toothbrush. Leave to dry in the shade.

SMOKE STAINS

Paint or Wood
Usually a solution of 1 cup (6 oz) washing soda in 5 litres of water will be sufficient to clean most smoke stains. Wash off with clean water. If necessary repeat. Do not attempt to paint over the soot as the tarry deposits in the soot will bleed through the paint. To overcome this, paint stain with shellac or aluminium paint after which ordinary paint may be used. However, wash first before any attempt to paint.
*Rub on a solution of starch and water or fullers earth and water. When dry wipe off and wash as usual.

SOAP MAKING

9 litres (40 cups) cold water
500 g (16 oz) caustic soda
375 g (12 oz) resin (roughly crushed)
11 cups (2.75 kg) clarified fat (salt free)
2/3 cup (3 oz) borax
1 cup (8 fl oz) kerosene

Pour the cold water and caustic soda into a 20 litre drum and bring to the boil, stirring occasionally with an extra long stick. AVOID THE FUMES CONTACTING THE SKIN, PARTICULARLY THE HANDS AND FACE, AND WATCH CONSTANTLY AS THIS MIXTURE BOILS OVER VERY QUICKLY. Keep a bottle of cold water handy and add a few drops if mixture begins to boil over.
When the water and caustic soda begin to boil, add the resin and stir well until dissolved. Add the fat and borax and, stirring occasionally, bring back to the boil. Reduce temperature to half and simmer vigorously for 1½ hours, stirring occasionally. You may have to reduce the temperature even further to stop the mixture boiling over and then increase it again as required. The mixture should start to thicken approximately 30 minutes after it re-boils following the addition of the fat. When cooking is completed, remove from heat, add the kerosone, stir well and pour into moulds. Do not use aluminium moulds. Leave to set overnight. Next day cut the soap into bars or tablets and leave to harden for 6 or more weeks before using. **CAUTION ▶**
The finished soap is light fawn in colour with a faint soapy aroma, however you can adjust this by adding to the mixture after it is removed from the heat and prior to adding the kerosene, approximately 1 tablespoon of any food colouring you prefer and approximately 6 teaspoons of an essential oil essence of your choice. These are available from health food stores.
If you happen to overboil the mixture with a resultant loss in volume, rectify by adding sufficient water to bring it back to its original volume and re-boil for a further 10 minutes.

SOOT Chimney

Put ordinary zinc onto a well lit and blazing fire. The chemical vapour absorbs the soot and it goes out the chimney.

SPECTACLES

A little vinegar on a clean cloth will make spectacles gleam.
*Mix together ½ cup (4 fl oz) of methylated spirits and 2 teaspoons of glycerine and store in a small bottle. To use, sprinkle a few drops onto a soft cloth and then clean and polish the spectacles. The glycerine will help prevent the spectacles going misty. **CAUTION ▶**

SPIRITS

See ALCOHOL (SPIRITS) (page 8).

STICKING PLASTER RESIDUE

Polished Wood
Remove marks with kerosene and rub over area with vinegar. Dry off and apply furniture polish.

Skin
Rub with cloth dipped in kerosene.

STOVE TOP/HOT PLATES

While warm, clean all over with vinegar and steel wool. Wipe dry with warm water and sponge.

SUITS OR TROUSERS

Shiny
To 2½ cups (20 fl oz) of warm water add 1 teaspoon of ammonia. Sponge solution well into shiny suit or trousers and iron with a damp cloth.
For dark clothing which is not too shiny, use strained cold tea for wetting the dampening cloth and iron as usual.

TAR

Car Paintwork
Rub gently with eucalyptus oil.

Hands
Rub well with lard.

Linen or Cotton
Spread butter on stain then stretch fabric over a pad made from rags. Dab on a small amount of hydrochloric acid and rub around stain until it is absorbed by the pad. Wash off in petrol and then wash in usual way. **CAUTION ▶**

Wool
Dab on glycerine and leave to soak for 1 hour. Wash off with wool detergent and rinse as usual.

TARNISH

Brass
Make the following solution:
¼ cup (2 fl oz) vinegar
1 tablespoon lemon juice
1 teaspoon salt

Apply solution with fine steel wool in one direction only. Do not rub crosswise or in circles. Let stand for 20 minutes. Rinse clean and dry.
On fine filigree, apply solution with an old toothbrush or paintbrush. Small items can be left soaking in the solution for 20 minutes. Wash off with hot soapy water, rinse in clean water and dry.
*For severe tarnish, use a solution of 1 part hydrochloric acid to 5 parts water. **CAUTION ▶**

Apply with an old brush. Wash off with hot soapy water, rinse in clean water and dry.

See BRASS (page 13).

Copper
Mix equal quantities of kerosene and bicarbonate of soda (baking soda) and rub all over the copper, in straight lines, with fine steel wool. Do not rub crosswise or in circles. Wash off with hot soapy water, rinse in clean water and dry. **CAUTION ▶**

See COPPER (page 21).

Silver

See SILVER (page 66).

TEA

Carpet
Mix borax with warm water and rub affected area with cloth dipped in this solution.
* Spread a little glycerine over stain and leave for 4 hours. Sponge off with methylated spirits. **CAUTION ▶**

China
Rub well with powdered whiting or salt.

Cotton or Linen
Ensure first that fabric will withstand boiling water.
Spread stained area over saucepan or similar and, from a height of ½ to 1 metre, pour through it boiling water. When stain is removed wash as usual.
If stain is old spread on a mixture of 1 teaspoon borax and 2½ cups (20 fl oz) water. Leave for 15 minutes and wash as usual.

Marble

See COFFEE, Marble (page 20).

Vacuum Bottle
Make a solution of ⅓ cup (2 oz) bicarbonate of soda (baking soda) to 2½ cups (20 fl oz) boiling water. Pour into vacuum bottle and shake well. Leave for 10 minutes. Wash as usual.

Woollens
Mix glycerine with egg yolk, spread over stain and leave for 30 minutes. Wash in warm water.

TEAPOTS

Aluminium
Fill teapot with boiling water, add 2 teaspoons of cream of tartar, stir and leave for 4 to 5 hours. Remove any white residue with soap and fine steel wool. Rinse well.

China
Moisten a cloth with methylated spirits, dip in whiting and rub on the inside of teapot. Wash and rinse thoroughly.
CAUTION ▶

Silver
Fill teapot with boiling water, add 1 tablespoon of borax and 3 drops of bleach. Cover teapot with a tea towel and let stand for 2 or 3 hours. Wash and rinse thoroughly. Do not allow solution to spill onto the outside as it could damage the silver.
*Mix 2 teaspoons each of bicarbonate of soda (baking soda), flour and vinegar together and rub on the inside of teapot. Leave overnight and then wash and rinse thoroughly.

TERAZZO

See FLOORS, TERAZZO (page 28).

TICK REPELLANT

In 5 tablespoons methylated spirits melt 3 x 7 g (1/4 oz) camphor tablets, mix well and apply to your pet's skin every 2 or 3 weeks. In badly infested areas apply every week. **CAUTION ▶**

TOBACCO

Marble

See COFFEE, Marble (page 20).

Odour
Pour 1 tablespoon of ammonia in a small bowl and leave overnight in the centre of the room. **CAUTION ▶**

Prevent Odour
Cover bottom of each ash tray with bicarbonate of soda (baking soda).

UPHOLSTERY

See CHAIR UPHOLSTERY (page 17).

URINE

Carpet
Absorb as much urine as possible then sprinkle area with warm water. Follow this by sponging area with a solution of equal parts of detergent and warm water and a half part of vinegar. Pat dry and repeat sponging with solution 2 or 3 times. Finally sponge with clean water and pat dry. At no time saturate the carpet.

Washables
Sponge stain with a little liquid ammonia and let soak for a few minutes. Rinse and wash as usual. **CAUTION ▶**

VACUUM FLASKS

Musty
Put 1 tablespoon of sugar in the flask and three quarters fill with boiling water. Replace lid, shake a few times and leave for 30 minutes. Empty and rinse well in cold water.

VEIL WHITE BRIDAL

Storing
To maintain the whiteness of a bridal veil, before storing it, rinse well in an extra strong solution of blue. When dry, place wax paper over it and press with a warm iron.
If the veil is bulky put it in a plastic bag, blow up the bag and seal with a rubber band.

VINYL

See LINOLEUM OR VINYL (page 46).

VOMIT

Carpet and Unwashables

Pick up with rags as much vomit as possible. Sponge with diluted liquid detergent and pat dry. When completely dry and if any stain remains sponge with methylated spirits. **CAUTION ▶**

Odour

Make a weak solution of bicarbonate of soda (baking soda) and water and sponge onto affected area.

WALLPAPER

General Purpose Cleaner

Mix together *1½ cups (6 oz) of plain (all-purpose) flour, 6 teaspoons of household ammonia, 1 teaspoon bicarbonate of soda (baking soda) and sufficient cold water to make a stiff dough*. Place in a bowl and steam for 1 hour. Knead well and leave for an hour or so. To clean wallpaper, rub with pieces of the dough. **CAUTION ▶**
*Rub marks gently with stale bread or an art gum eraser.

WATER MARKS

Carpet

Do not let water dry but as quickly as possible absorb it with a sponge. Then, if possible, prop carpet up to let air circulate and place near it an electric heater or fan. When dry remove any stains with a detergent solution of a proprietary brand of carpet cleaner.

Furniture

Rub well into the polished wood some petroleum jelly or camphorated oil. Keep rubbing until marks disappear.

Silk or Velvet

Hold fabric over steam for a few seconds and pat dry.

Suede

When spots are dry, remove them by rubbing with a soft pencil eraser or by rubbing the spots against another part of the suede material.

Unpainted Wood

Use a proprietary brand of wood bleach in which the use of two liquids is employed.
*Place 3 or 4 sheets of blotting paper over stain and press with a fairly warm iron. Repeat until stain is removed.

WAX

Clothes

Place clean blotting paper over wax and press with a hot iron. Remove remaining smear with methylated spirits.
CAUTION ▶

See CANDLE GREASE (page 15).

Floor

Scrub floor with a mixture of ½ cup (4 fl oz) ammonia and ½ cup (4 fl oz) detergent to 5 litres of hot water. Wait until completely dry before applying new wax.
CAUTION ▶

WINE

Carpet

As quickly as possible absorb excess liquid then sprinkle over a liberal amount of talcum powder. Replace powder as it becomes wet. Sponge with clean water and pat dry. If still stained, sponge with diluted liquid detergent or glycerine followed in 30 minutes by clean water. Pat dry.

Cotton or Linen

Ensure first that fabric will withstand boiling water.
Spread stained area over a saucepan or similar and from a height of ½ to 1 metre, pour through it boiling water. When stains are removed, wash as usual.
If stain is old, spread on a mixture of 2 teaspoons borax and 1¼ cups (10 fl oz) water. Leave for 15 minutes and wash as usual.

Wool, Rayon or Silk

Wet with cold water followed by glycerine. Allow 1 hour, then sponge with lemon juice. Rinse off.

WOODEN POLISHED FLOORS

See FLOORS, WOODEN POLISHED (page 28).

WOOLLENS

Mix well in a large screw top jar, the following:
2½ cups (10 oz) special wool soap powder
1¼ cups (10 fl oz) methylated spirits
¼ cup (2 fl oz) eucalyptus oil
¼ cup (2 fl oz) warm water

Gradually add the liquid ingredients to the powder.
Add ½ cup (4 fl oz) of the above mixture to 4.5 litres of warm water. Mix well and gently immerse woollens. Soak woollens for 10 minutes, then press and squeeze without rubbing, until clean. Finally hang to dry WITHOUT wringing. **CAUTION ▶**

Creamed
Dampen and sprinkle with powdered magnesia. Rub well in, roll up and put into a plastic bag. Leave for 10 hours and then rinse well and dry out of the sun.

Removing Knobs (Pilling)
Brush with a proprietary brand of flat plastic pot scourer.

YELLOW STAINS

See BLEACH, YELLOW (page 12).

INDEX